FISHING IN ASSYNT

An oral history by Dave McBain

Historic Assynt

ISBN 978-1-906804-61-9

Published by Historic Assynt © 2021

Compiled and edited by Dave McBain

Designed by Ronan Martin

Map by Ronan Martin

Front cover image: The Inverlossie UL 106 (John C. MacLeod)

Back cover image: Golden Emblem landing at Lochinver, 1960s (Jean McBain)

Title page image: the alternative fish market, 1980s (Nick Groves)

Printed by J Thomson Colour Printers

This project was completed as part of the
Coigach & Assynt Living Landscape Partnership (CALLP) Scheme.

This project has only been possible with the generous support
from the above organisations.

With grateful thanks to:

Alan MacLeod, Alex McBain, Angus MacKenzie, Boyd Alexander, Bruce MacKenzie, Gordon Sleight, Graeme Cavers, Gwen Richards, Hector MacKenzie, Ian MacLeod, Jean McBain, Jen Harland, Jimmy Gault, Jimmy Peat, Joan Hutchison, John C. MacLeod, John Thompson, Katherine Anderson, Ken Fairchild, Malcolm Bangor-Jones, Morag MacLennan, Murdo Aird, Murray Campbell, Nick Groves, Roy MacLeod, Sandra Callus, Susan Templeton, Willie Hutchison, Willie MacLeod, Vida Smith, Wilma MacKay and Wilma MacLeod.

For their time, memories, photographs and feedback.

Preface

This is a book of memories told as they are remembered – others may recall differently. Some may wonder why one gem or another is missing and it is only hoped they will share those stories with us also.

The project came directly from a series of conversations with friends and family about the harbour and the realisation that so many people who we fondly remember are no longer with us – and from there came a desire to preserve at least some of the memories of a time past. As the son of a fisherman (and as no-one else was volunteering) I have attempted to write down the memories of those who still had them.

A total of 18 interviews with fishers, their families, harbour workers, office workers and drivers were conducted over the course of 2020-21 and have been hopefully woven together into a timeline covering the growth of the industry.

Dave McBain
Lochinver, August 2021

Contents

Introduction

When the winds are howling, and the waves are surging there can be no more welcome sight than the harbour lights and somewhere to tie up for the night. For those of us tucked up in a warm house looking out the window it may be difficult to comprehend the relief of making it safely back to somewhere you could rest for a few hours. The relief those lights would bring to fishers as they approached must have been immense.

The life of a fisherman is one that would make for nightmares in many people's minds – working night and day on a sea that rises and falls in a constantly moving swell. Whether it be a gentle roll or a thump between waves, the sea will rarely be still.

Safe harbour (credit: Michael Rochester)

Rough seas were a fact of life (credit: Morag MacLennan)

As one local fisher recalled his first week at the sea as a young teenager was out of Kinlochbervie. A friend also worked on the boat and his pal's father had driven up on the Friday to take the two youngsters' home for the weekend.

Having gone straight from boat to car as they landed, his first foray on dry land was when the car stopped to wait for the ferry at Kylesku. After a week at sea, he was unused to the steadiness of the dry land.

As he walked down the slipway, he heard a call from a stationary car "Not sure what's wrong with that lad, but it looks like he's practising for walking on the moon".

He soon gained his sea legs.

Sharing a cabin with your crewmates, mostly too exhausted to remove anything except their oilskins and to be honest smelling fairly rank was just part of the life. As for the food – well sometimes that was surprisingly good. Some of the part time cooks on those boats would put many a chef to shame.

Exhaustion and camaraderie went hand-in-hand with the fisherman's life and for those new to the trade it would be common enough to throw in a measure of seasickness. Though rewards could be good, they were always hard-earned by a remarkable group of people.

Long hours and hard work built strong friendships and crews were regularly in touch with one another over the boat radios sharing news, occasionally gossip and most importantly weather updates.

The friendships between men who were essentially trade rivals remain exceptionally strong. I cannot, for example, imagine supermarket staff (to pick just one industry at random) attending the funeral of an unrelated colleague from another business in another town, but I have seen on many occasions skippers and crew cross from one end of the country to another to say a final farewell to an old rival in trade.

I can recall from my own childhood, crew from various boats popping over to my parents' house to spend an evening in front of the fire rather than in the chill of the boat and sharing news well on into the night. With a father who never smoked and rarely drank, it was not at all unusual that friends would arrive with all they needed for a blether – including the ashtray.

It wasn't just in Lochinver that people fished. Smaller boats operated – and still do – around the coast of Assynt from harbours such as Nedd, Kylesku and Culkein Drumbeg. There was a thriving salmon fishery at Clachtoll and Culkein Achnacarnin as well as shellfish and seaweed fishing from the shore all around the coast.

What we have now is a shadow of the trade it once was and we are in danger of forgetting the buzz on the harbour, the excitement of a fish market and the wonderful characters who worked on the boats, on the harbour and in some cases were just there – with the most of us, even at the time, unsure of what they did.

Landing (credit: Morag MacLennan)

A well-known song lyric says, "those days are past now, and in the past, they must remain", but the aim of this book is to capture some of the memories, some of the stories and if possible, just an essence of the life and verve of our seafaring past.

The historical record will in years to come almost certainly include the number of boxes landed and the prices fish raised, but it is unlikely to tell us very much of the people who fished from the harbour in what eventually became Lochinver. Hopefully, this publication will address this in a small way.

Interviewing fishermen, harbour workers and office staff we trace a recent history of the port from the fishing boom of the 1950s-1970, through to the arrival of continental trawlers and the gradual decline of the Scottish fishing industry.

This book covers, for the most part, the oral history of commercial sea fishing in Assynt. For freshwater angling, there is a lovely publication by Cathel MacLeod which covers the lochs and rivers.[1] This study has focussed on Seine, Trawl, Creels and Bag netting of Salmon with a shout to the Seaweed fishing that ran alongside them.

Individual interviews have been mixed on a timeline to provide flow rather than shared in full. Unless from a written work, or tales involve the individual telling it, citations have been deliberately omitted.

It is an oral history and tells the story as folk remember it – whether others will remember it in the same way might be interesting to find out, but it is those memories we have that we will share.

There were of course many who fished long before living memory and it is important to give a voice to those and to build a picture of where those others came from.

---

[1] Cathel MacLeod, "Trout Fishing in Assynt", Scottish Country Sports Tourism Group: Trochry, 2007

Early records

The first evidence we have for fishing in Assynt came from Clachtoll broch where both molluscs – which may have been used for food or bait – and fish bones were recovered.[2] The remains recovered included both freshwater and seawater species, but generally all were species which might have been caught from the rocks. It is likely that fishing was a long-established practice by the iron age but Clachtoll broch provides the first proven evidence we have.

Unsurprisingly there is little by the way of written records for some centuries after the broch burned to the ground around 50BC.

Eilean Assynt, Ardvreck and the Cam loch structure were all surrounded by water, suggesting that the ready supply of fish surrounding the structures would have provided for the residents, but there is no written record to support this.

Information we do have is from various old maps from the Sixteenth century onwards which note the point of Stoer and "Allerot" round about where Lochinver is now. The point of Stoer is obvious, both in its visibility from the sea and as many would testify the danger to shipping from the surrounding coast. Allerot though raises more questions – was it a port that ships visited or just a point visible from the sea? Maps would suggest that it was around where Baddidarroch is today, but they were far from accurate.

There have been suggestions that it might be a mishearing of Ardroe or based on the old name for the River Inver – the "Abrud".[3] Based on the map locations, this writer's personal feeling is that the latter is more likely.

---

2 Harland, J (2021), "Clachtoll broch: fish remains", unpublished at time of writing

Excerpt from Blome, Richard (1673), *A Mapp of the Kingdome of Scotland / by Ric. Blome; R. Palmer, sculp.* Reproduced with the permission of the National Library of Scotland

The fact that they appear on centuries old maps opens the possibility of a safe harbour, a centre of trade and the likelihood of boats landing their catches there.

The earliest record found in this publication was from Bailie Stuart's letter books which reports the 1723 purchase of herring from Mrs MacKenzie of Assynt.[4] Unfortunately where in Assynt is not mentioned, but it indicates that herring were being caught and sold on a commercial basis.

Culag has existed since at least the mid 1700s when it appeared on General Roy's map and John Home's maps, but in both cases the significant building listed was a mill.

3 Malcolm Bangor-Jones, *Historic Assynt*, The Assynt press, 2008
4 William MacKay, "Industrial Life in the Highlands in Olden Time", in "Home life of the Highlanders 1400-1746", David Norman MacKay, Mackelhose (1911)

We can reasonably assume that fishing was taking place from the earliest of times, but the historical record is thin on the ground. However, in 1773 John MacIver (Depute Judiciary Baillie on the North West Coast of Scotland) journals describe "plentifull herring fishing and Compact little fleet & a Vast manny Country Boats".[5]

On a return visit three years later in 1776 he recorded sixty-four vessels fishing from Loch Nedd in December – though the record does not record whether these were local boats or not.[6] It is likely there would have been a mix or larger boats from further South being supplied by local small boats - the 'Country Boats'. These caught fish for local consumption and sold fish to the large vessels. MacIver may have counted craft rather than distinguish between the two.

In 1775 there are records of a herring station opening at Culag which marks the beginnings of an ongoing historical record of the port. The date is significantly one year after Holmes' survey, so whether population moved to newly created jobs or not is intriguing.

The herring station was built by Donald Ross and Company for a sum of £3000 and included smoking houses that were able to smoke 1,000 barrels of fish at a time.[7] A herring barrel in Scotland would have held 66 Scots pints (equivalent to an English Quart) – roughly 12 gallons/55 litres.[8] If processing for 1000 barrels was present, then there would have been some significant structures in place.

The site processed white herring (pickled in salt) and red (smoked) herring which were shipped to Liverpool and onwards from there to Spain, Portugal and the Caribbean. Ross employed 47 boats, each with a crew of five, though we cannot be certain if these were locally crewed. There were also 80 to 100 people employed onshore in processing the fish. The scale of this enterprise with up to 250 people employed, possibly eclipsed even the 1970s in terms of labour – though it should be noted that there was a short herring season and no records of whether employees were retained over the rest of the year and other fish were processed during those periods.

---

[5] Malcolm Bangor-Jones, "18th Century Herring Fishing", Am Bratach, October 2006 Original source National records of Scotland E727/18
[6] Ibid
[7] Malcolm Bangor-Jones – Historic Assynt
[8] Zupko, R. (1977). The Weights and Measures of Scotland before the Union. *The Scottish Historical Review, 56*(162), 119-145.

The business reported "considerable problems" with the customs house on Isle Martin over salt sales which would have been vital as part of the preservation process. It was soon sold to Roderick Morrison of Stornoway (owner of the similar station on Tanera) and his partner John Mackenzie before being sold again to Donald MacDonald of Skibost in the 1790s who had handed the business over to his son by the time the artist William Daniell visited in 1820 and reported a "whole scene of bustle and hustle".[9]

Landing records suggest Culag, Tanera, Isle Martin and Ullapool were all a similar size. The station at Ullapool reportedly had 72 smoking fires running all day every day – although this was seasonal work, which would have been labour and wood intensive. It is assumed that wood fuel would have been brought in by return from boats shipping the herring out.[10]

MacDonald added a cannery to the smokehouse in the 1830s, which must have been one of the earliest in the country. Canning as a process appears to have started around the time of the Spanish/Portuguese peninsular war and the reported red roof on the cannery – matching the Ullapool customs house has been suggested were Portuguese tiles used as ballast on returning herring shipments before the building was put up. It is more likely that they were pantiles from the South of Scotland. The cannery was producing canned fish, venison and locally produced soup.[11]

Unfortunately, the business appears to have failed when MacDonald fled the country to avoid criminal proceedings over "unpaid bills" in the mid-1840s.[12]

Around the same time as the development of the herring station at Culag, both the Highland clearances and the Napoleonic wars were taking place. Cleared farms, people needing work and a war led to a demand for saltpetre which is a derivative of kelp and there are records

---

9 Aymee Thorne, "A journey through Sutherland", extract from Assynt Old Kirk records – no citation on document
10 Cathy Dagg, Red fish presentation, Ullappol harbour offices, 2019
11 Malcolm Bangor-Jones, Historic Assynt, The Assynt press: Dundee, 2008, p16
12 Ibid and Cathy Dagg, *Red herrings presentation*, Ullapool, 2019

of kelp harvesting in the parish – sadly in many cases these come from oral records of fishers drowning and from local protests due to the kelp being needed to fertilise the poor ground and having tenancy agreements altered to ensure they collected it as a saleable resource.[13]

There are still the remains of a fish trap in the centre of the village in Lochinver. It has been suggested it was built in the 1820s to 30s, but the construction date is unknown, and the type of trap has been in use for over 1000 years. The later date is based on a belief that the fish trap may have supplemented the boats for the herring processing. Older residents refer to it as a Carraidh (pronounced 'carry') and similar traps were referred to as Yares. The idea of these is simple – a wall or fence forms a rough semi-circle or V shape which at high tide fish could swim over, but as the tide fell, they would be forced to either swim out through a netted gap or remain trapped in the centre. Whether it was used for herring or salmon is very much lost to history, but the one in Lochinver is a serious piece of construction and must have been well used for a period – whether it was ten or a thousand years – the technology is old enough for either.

The Lochinver Carraidh has been out of use since before anyone I spoke to can remember, but it has trapped fish in living memory. The last one I know of being a "decent sized" salmon brought home by a primary schoolboy in the early 1960s which he recovered from the shallows in the middle of the trap.

There is a similar but smaller trap in Nedd and possibly another in in Loch Roe.

Curiously James Loch's 1820 account of improvements on the Sutherland estate reference cod rather than herring fishing – "The number of boats belonging to Assynt engaged in cod fishing, amount to seventy-eight manned with six men each". Noting the fishing season was from March to July and fish being sold for two pence apiece and that a prize was given to each of the three most successful boats in the area.[14]

---

[13] Malcolm Bangor-Jones, The Assynt Clearances, he Assynt press: Dundee, 2001, p26
[14] James Loch, An account of the improvements on the estates of the Marquis of Stafford in the counties of Stafford and Salop and on the Estate of Sutherland, 1820 – extract held in Assynt Archive, Old Kirk, Inchnadamph

It is of course possible that Loch's visit coincided with the cod fishing season and that those same boats would, a few month later have been landing herring. Cod fishing was something pursued by the Sutherland estate and Loch's account might reflect that pursuit.

The period also coincided with a period where local fisherman began to buy shares in larger boats that could take them round to the East Coast Herring Fishing – particularly out of Wick. Some of course merely walked and became hired hands. Census returns also suggest crews from east coast ports such as Buckie also came and based themselves on the West coast, staying at places like Oldany Island and Handa and "bringing a woman with them to cook".[15]

By 1869, a significant number of local residents were employed in the herring fishing industry and following the fleet around the coast. A 2006 'Am Bratach' article describing losses of life and craft after a particularly severe storm notes 200 men from twenty-seven Assynt townships fishing from Wick – producing around treble the income of local lobster fishing.[16] Notably some of these fishers were from the inland settlements as well as from the coastal communities.

Summary data from the article is shown overpage.

Perhaps notable is that the article shows housing of various types in each township as well as the number of men fishing.

Also notable is that the towns of Filin and Inver (which today make up Lochinver) appeared much less active than they went on to become.

By the late 1890s there was sufficient fishing trade that consideration was being given to a railway line into Lochinver, though a letter to the Scotsman from the headmaster of Loretto school in Musselburgh and regular holiday visitor to Strathan which opposed the scheme drew attention to the cost as well as the "small inadequate harbour and its too well-known to be dangerous approach (as its history of shipwrecks proves)".[17] The account also discusses the damage being done by dredging the bottom by trawl netters – a theme which will recur in this volume.

---

15 Malcolm Bangor-Jones, pers comms
16 Roger Leitch, "the case of Assynt", Am Bratach January 2006
17 H. L. Almond, "Railway travelling in the Highlands", letter to The Scotsman, 17th September 1894

Men fishing in Wick 1869 by township

Township	Number of houses with chimneys	Slated houses	Huts	Hired men in Wick
Nedd	9	-	20	12
Drumbeg	11	3	13	23
Culkein Drumbeg	16	2	10	15
Oldney	-	2	2	-
Clashnessie	13	3	17	19
Achnacarnin	12	-	5	16
Culkeine Achnacarnin	25	2	7	12
Clashmore	20	-	25	40
Balchaidich	6	1	8	6
Stoer	17	5	9	8
Clachtoll	16	-	17	11
Achmeloie	17	1	26	8
Ardroe	3	-	3	4
Torbreck	6	1	1	2
Baddanock	9	-	2	2
Inver	6	1	-	-
Felin	5	15	-	-
Strathan	9	1	3	8
Inverkirkaig	11	-	5	16
Badnaman	8	-	1	3
Brackloch	2	1	-	-
Kirkton Assynt	2	3	-	-
Inchnadamph	4	2	-	-
AltnaKealgach	1	1	-	-
Elphin	14	2	12	-
Knockan	11	-	7	-
Unapool	6	1	4	-
Totals	**259**	**47**	**187**	**200**

Lochinver — 1890

This photograph   of a part of Lochinver village at an interesting point in its development, was probably taken about 1890. It was certainly prior to the building of the Free Presbyterian Church in 1897.

It is interesting to note the number of services provided by the village even in those days. It should be remembered that Lochinver was a fairly new village. In a reply to the then Board of Agriculture in 1810, the factor for Sutherland estate said "Various villages are not only in contemplation, but will, this season (1810) be commenced, namely, a maritime village at Lochinver in Assynt . . ."

Viewed from left to right, the picture shows Forbes' boarding house, then sheds where the Parkhouse Hotel and Lochinver Stores and the FP Church now stand. The set-back building known as the Transvaal still exists, as do the ruins of the old slaughter-house with its walled enclosure. The knot of folk are exchanging the news of the day in front of the village shop.

The police station and Tigh Lois, an early doctor's house, lead on to the Lodge, which at that time would be for shooting and fishing guests only. The pub was situated where the baker's house is today. There was also a small bakery next door in those days. People recall the daily spectacle of Dan the Baker, striding along with a board on his head loaded with many dozen loaves, using no hands, on his way to K P Mackenzie's Shop (where Caberfeidh Cafe is today).

Behind the Inn and Bakery can be seen the coach-house and stables for the mail and passenger run to Lairg. Moving along, there were several houses, including that of a shoemaker and a famous character, Murdo Kerr, fisherman, boat-hirer and, it is claimed, one not above a spot of contraband running on occasion. There is some uncertainty about the house at the present car-park, but the large building was the Mission Hall which also acted as a school for a period. The house in the foreground on the north side of the bay is Briar Cottage.

The village pump for the water supply for the houses was behind the shop. An undeveloped Cruamer Park can be seen in the distant right. To the south of the park in what is now the schoolhouse garden stood the village stocks, where law-breakers could be given corrective treatment.

A newspaper article showing Lochinver in 1890

An early image of the village was passed to me from a newspaper clipping, which unfortunately does not name the paper concerned. It is shared here in the spirit it was intended with apologies for a lack of a citation to the original paper.

The herring trade continued through until the World War 1 when many of the fishers went into the services and never returned to the trade.

It would also be remiss not to mention the supply ships which brought goods to the harbour for local shops.

Postcard image of the Clansman at Culag (credit: John C. MacLeod)

There was a story for which I have no written account that a night watchman on the clansman fell overboard and drowned at Culag shortly after World War I ended. There were rumours of a local man found on board the craft that evening looking to make off with goods, but no charges were ever brought.

One story from shortly before then is worthy of mention.

In 1902 someone learned that a church in Nairn was no longer required after a new kirk was built over there and a local committee led by James Gordon somehow negotiated with the Nairn congregation to take on their old building. The negotiations must have been a history in themselves, but the price paid was a boatload of peats in return for what is now Lochinver Church of Scotland.

The building was deconstructed, and each stone marked before local herring boats transported it round the Pentland firth and Cape Wrath before the building was rebuilt at its present site in Lochinver.

Church of Scotland in Lochinver Early twentieth century (credit: Susan Templeton)

The trade must be a story in itself – I cannot imagine it as anything other than a bar-room style negotiation. The deconstruction and re-building was a massive undertaking, particularly if you consider how many herring craft it would take to transport a building of that size. They would mostly be well under 50 feet in length. How many days would it take to sail round to Nairn and back again? When would the weather be good enough to allow this trip safely (almost certainly in the same months the herring were most active)? And of course, what wage would feed the crews family to compensate for that loss of income?

This was a huge project possibly in the peak earning months of the year and required multiple families to give so much. They were not the only ones to make a sacrifice for this undertaking – one local crofter paid the ultimate price when a piece of scaffold gave way and he fell to his death during the rebuild.

Joan Hutchison (nee Sutherland) and her sister Marlene recalled their father telling them that he began fishing with his father in 1923 at the age of 14 when they were fishing for herring and landing them on to a German "klondyker" (processing vessel).

Their father and grandfather were at times the only local fishers in Lochinver and the girls remember their father making his own fishboxes in the garden.

Culag Hotel, Lochinver.

Postcard showing Lochinver harbour in the 1920s (Postcard by A. MacKenzie, Lochinver courtesy of John C. MacLeod)

Lochinver Harbour 1950s (credit: John C. MacLeod)

The first pictorial evidence of the harbour comes from the 1920s, by which time the harbour entrance was stone built with a wooden pier at the front of the small hill in front of the Culag hotel. The hotel was devastated by fire in 1929 and the red roofed section of the building destroyed. The boats shown would have been herring drifters. Note the stone-built harbour to the left of the image has been extended and would have been where the road is now – the sheds that stand on that site now, are on top of that extension.

After the end of the First World War, there appears to have been a hiatus in fishing with a demise of the herring trade and a very gradual introduction of other local fishing before the Lochinver Fish Selling Company Ltd was active in the late 1940s but formally established as a business in 1956 after a period of expansion following the end of the Second World War.

One story from that period which is worth sharing involved a local man on active service just after the Second World War, as shared by John C. MacLeod:

When I was on the Golden Emblem, David told me he was doing National Service after the war in Germany. When on leave a group of them were in a bar for an evening out and a waiter heard them speaking and came and asked David where he was from.

He said a small place in North West Scotland, but you would never know.

"Oh, but I might" said the waiter.

David said a small place in North West Scotland called Lochinver expecting that to be the end of that conversation.

The German said, I know it very well, he described the mountains, the village and the islands of Soyea and A' Chleit.

"I was a U-Boat captain during the war and we used to charge our batteries there" he said, "we used to hide in the big hole behind the islands down to ninety fathoms, five hundred and forty feet deep".

John knew the spot well as a friend had lost a set of his trawl doors in the same hole.

Lochinver Fish Selling
Early years

Lochinver Fish Selling (LFS) originally started in a small office in the centre of Lochinver – in what is at the time of writing the Coffee Shop but at the time was the registrar's office.

George Mackay and Christie Campbell with the first two Lochinver Fish Selling lorries (credit: John C. MacLeod)

The business was the brainchild of Hector Mackay. Hector was the registrar of births, marriages and deaths for the parish but soon after arriving in Lochinver from Strathy, developed an interest in fishing. He was particularly troubled by the dangers of boats hitting the rocks coming into Lochinver bay and his daughter-in-law recalled he was regularly seen in the early years of the business standing on the pier with a lantern to guide boats in. Unsurprisingly harbour lighting was one of the issues addressed quite early in the company's lifespan.

The harbour – like much of the parish – was owned by the Vestey family until it was purchased by the Highland council towards the end of the twentieth century. Much of the early negotiations for harbour improvement would have been done with the local estate.

From the start LFS was a mix of a small chandlery business and an office handling sales and boat management. The cramped registrar's office was, of course, far too small for the business and almost from its formation he was looking for alternative premises. In particular, the premises were too small for much of the equipment boats required and the early days of LFS are fondly remembered as using every shed, garage and piece of waste ground available as "temporary" storage for equipment. Ian "Nurse" MacLeod recalled ropes piled on pallets on the hill above his house and the wash house building being filled with gear. In fact, any piece of ground, shed that could be begged or borrowed was put to some use.

The old lime store was occasionally a chandlery store also (credit: John C. MacLeod)

This was supported by the County council who purchased land at the junction with Stoer road to store fish boxes away from the harbour area where the landowner feared they would impact on views from his harbourside hotel.

The first employee of LFS was Nan MacLeod from Stoer, who had previously worked as a fish buyer in Glasgow. Her contacts were a key part of building the business alongside Hector and son George's efforts to tempt east coast fishers into using the port.

Joan Hutchison recalled that along with councillor Donald McBain, Hector Mackay pressed the council for land to build houses which would support East coast fishers to settle in Lochinver. This was to some extent achieved, but the drawback of no local high school and secondary school children having to board on the East coast to complete their education meant that few settled in the area.

Many of the buyers were able to pick up fish in Lochinver at what they considered a "knock down" price, compared to other ports, and they commonly took them to other ports where they would be resold for a higher price. Typical destinations were Banff, Buckie or Aberdeen.

One local buyer earned the nickname Christy "Buckie" MacKenzie over his belief that the best prices for fish could be found at the East coast port, so he would buy at Lochinver and arrange transport East for them to be re-sold in Buckie. He carved a successful career in doing so.

In the early days of the harbour, the prices for plaice were higher than most other species and therefore a haul of plaice was prized. So prized that whilst most other fish was transported by fish lorry to its eventual destination, boxes of plaice were sent on the mail bus to Lairg for onwards transportation by train directly to the bigger cities.

The mail bus driver Donald "the mail" MacKenzie was of course a part-time fisherman himself, so would have had his own connections in that piece of the sales picture.

Drivers to a man, noted that some destinations were never liked (e.g. Leith) as skimming fish (taking a few from each box for their own boxes – to be sold privately) was common and openly practised. Although it didn't affect them directly, there was a professional pride in knowing that they completed the job they were paid for.

Due to Nan Macleod's connections in Glasgow initially much of Lochinver's fish went to the South of the country. The travel distance meant that buyers were keen to get their fish early to be on the road to ensure their load was delivered in good time to be resold in the morning market. Prices were accordingly always higher before 9pm – some of the smarter local buyers soon worked this out and gained a reputation for arriving towards the end of the market when there was less competition and lower prices.

LFS didn't have a monopoly in the early days. A rival business was run from the offices next to the "ranch" – the offices below the old Culag hotel staff quarters which at the time of writing are used by the Coigach and Assynt Living Landscape Project (CALLP) – were run by a company called Duthies.

Harbour equipment was scarce in the early days before the port was developed, but Joan Hutchison recalled a "fire cannon" being kept in a shed at the pier specifically because it was believed this is where it would be most needed. The device was operated by a hand pump which sucked in sea water and fired it out in a steady stream from the other side.

In particular, she recalled the fire which eventually destroyed the Lodge hotel (where the police station stands today) in 1950 and people running to the harbour to collect the fire cannon and hauling it across the village only to discover with flames engulfing the building, that the tide was out and the inlet pipe wasn't long enough to reach a feed of sea water to put out the fire.

Sadly, the hotel was lost on that night.

Early image showing the Lodge on the corner at the centre of the image (credit: Susan Templeton)

A huge part of the growth of LFS was George MacKay's skill in cajoling East coast skippers to base themselves out of Lochinver rather than other West coast ports. In some ways they were an easy target – the growing fishing industry in the Moray ports meant that there was a degree of overcrowding and harbour space was at a premium. Skippers including John Thompson had been actively considering fishing in the Minch but were reticent due to the lack of facilities on the West coast at the time.

John recalled being told that Lochinver was a herring port before the First World War, but that the industry had collapsed between the wars leaving the port struggling. By the time John arrived in Lochinver the port was largely a white fish port though one or two (for example Jimmy Young) were still pursuing herring in season.

John recalled up to 90 boats landing in Buckie on occasion which in a small harbour led to congestion and a feeling that stocks were being impacted. Several boats were looking to base themselves elsewhere and between distribution challenges and a lack of facilities he ended up first in Ullapool before being tempted to base the boat in Lochinver due largely to George Mackay's promises to develop the port and ensure the facilities the boat needed (ice, transport, chandlery) were all available to the boats landing here.

Over time through the 1950s and 1960s, two patterns went hand in hand. As larger boats were cajoled to begin landing at the harbour with bigger nets, better equipment (including mechanical winches) and greater efficiencies of scale, the smaller local craft found themselves less and less competitive. As owners retired, they were never replaced. This pattern would repeat itself in the 1980s and 1990s when state-sponsored decommissioning began.

AN ASIDE ON CRAFT SIZES

Willie Hutchison recalled that there were a lot of small boats around and that he had worked on one called the Luna del Mar (Rory Cathel and Donnie MacKaskill's boat) fishing out of Kirkaig. He recalled that Rory had served on a larger craft – an ocean liner - by the same name and named this one in tribute. Coincidentally, it the same boat that Willie and his wife Joan had travelled on when they returned from living in South Africa.

He recounted with a smile, the Luna del Mar fishing some way from home in the Pentland firth and being hit with engine issues. He couldn't recall the exact issue, but the engine was working but nowhere near capacity. They dutifully radio called in to Scrabster harbour that they were fine, but to put the lifeboat on standby in case it completely packed in.

The harbourmaster looked up the craft, assumed that it was the liner and cleared a huge space for its arrival only for a tiny 30 odd foot boat to limp its way into port some hours later.

Lochinver harbour 1950s (credit: John C. MacLeod)

In the early days, the boats were ring netting and John Thompson recalled that the Jeannie Mackay from Helmsdale was the first boat to try the larger seine net in the mid 1960s - a technique copied from Danish fishers.[18]

Jeannie MacKay (centre) was the first boat to fish seine from Lochinver (credit: John C. MacLeod)

---

[18] RD Galbraith and A. Rice, An introduction to commercial fishing gear and methods used in Scotland, Scotttish Executive, 2004 available online

Seine netting or purse seine involved connecting a dahn (or marker) buoy to one end of a coil of rope with the net at the other. Gradually the boat would steam away from the dahn buoy laying out rope and then net (the other end of the purse shaped net being attached to a second rope) before circling around and returning to the dahn and hauling the net back in. For most of the time the net would be hanging in the water usually some distance above the bottom.[19]

An early tale of interest involved the Guiding Star skippered by Donald Patience. Donald was a determined fisher and contemporaries recalled a time when he had injured his back but refused to stop fishing while he waited for treatment.

One fisher recalls him literally crawling on the deck, such was the pain he was in at the time.

The story however is one of his own, from a book he wrote in 2010:

In June 1952 the boat had been fishing from Ullapool but were heading up for Handa and around 4pm spotted something with a head like a seal but a neck possibly three feet long above the surface of the water.

After diverting closer the crew decided to lasso it. The venture was unsuccessful, but they were close enough, as it dived down and later resurfaced, to note that it was 18-20 feet long with a large flipper on either side and a greyish black colour.

Another boat the Margueritte came close as she had seen them circling and thought they may have lost someone overboard.

Donald was never a believer in tales of the loch Ness monster – claiming to be far too cynical, but he was sure he and the crew saw something that day. Whatever they saw, it's not something anyone has seen since, but the mysteries of the deep are just that - wonderfully mysterious.[20]

---

19   David Thompson, "The Seine net", Fishing news books:London 1969
20   Donald Patience, "Skippers Yarns from Avoch", For the right reasons: Inverness, 2010

Tudor Rose - Dahn being cast (credit: John C. MacLeod)

Olive Leaf - Seine netting note dahn buoys on the deck (credit: John C. MacLeod)

Seine netting was very successful for some time, but it was labour intensive. Both crew and skippers however would describe it as a truer and more skilful form of fishing. John C. MacLeod noted the picking of a suitable "room" (area to cast the net) and ensure that the tide or local current was flowing into the net as it lay in the water was a hugely skilled exercise and determining the right number of coils of rope to lay out for the room you were working was an art – by comparison "the trawl was boring".

The downside of seine fishing was that crew were perpetually feeding out rope or hauling it in and there was little rest time. Between all of the rope work any catches had to be graded, boxed and iced.

It was not unknown though, for a crew to take a short break from the netting to indulge in a bit of hand line fishing just to vary the day. Perhaps the joys of working a hand-line hearken back to a past form of fishing everyone enjoyed.

Gradually through the 1970s and 1980s the seine net was replaced by the trawl. This technique was less intensive on the crew though less kind to the environment – the net being simply dragged behind the boat with rollers (or "hoppers") running along the seabed. The trawl was preferred by some fishers for its ease of use, but criticised by others as it would scoop up all fish (including younger ones) as the mesh contracted whilst being dragged behind and did some considerable damage to breeding grounds on the bottom.

Fishers were never wasteful if it could be avoided, and local skippers would keep any dead undersized fish to be shared with creel fishers as bait.

Trawl net being hauled in (credit: John C. MacLeod)

A huge risk associated with the trawl was the greater risk of snagging the net on a rock at the bottom and ripping it. Fishers with net mending skills were always sure of a berth on boats and were hugely valued – almost as much as a skipper who knew the channels where it was safe to trawl. Over time hoppers (rollers which lift the net over obstacles on the seabed) improved, and more and more ground could be exploited.

At least one fisher noted that the big difference with trawling was that a net would be trawled for miles at a time whereas the seine net was fished in a much smaller enclosed space (a room).

With no comment made on the ecological effects, it was made very clear that the quantity of fish scooped up over the longer distances would be more damaging to stocks in the longer term.

Net mending skills were in great demand (credit: Jean McBain)

Whilst fishing technique changed, the biggest changes were taking place on the harbour. The Mackay family had promised several skippers that facilities would be built if they came. They were true to their word. A harbour extension in 1951 and an ice plant built in partnership with the Vestey family with numerous sheds built on the approach to the harbour over the next decade or two. Outside the walled gates to the Culag hotel, a fuel tank was installed.

Harbour in 1963 (credit: John C. MacLeod)

The ice plant being built was the site of one of Ian MacLeod's many stories. The Vestey family were partners in the building of the ice plant and had a remit for its maintenance as well. The plant had fairly simple mechanics – water came in, frozen in a sheet and flaked before being left chilled until it was required. There was very little that could go wrong in the process except that the stored ice if it melted a little would start to clump together and eventually would form an ice ball that was too large to get through the hatch and be fed on to waiting boats. The solution was simple – you went in with a shovel and broke it up.

Of course, breaking ice was cold, wet and unpleasant so was never a job to be relished. Which of course was why George MacKay would phone over to the estate factors office and begin the standard conversation opener.

"You are co-owners of this plant and my lads have been in there three or four times already this week breaking the ice up – it's about time the estate crew took their share of the work and put in a shift".

Ian recalled listening in on a few of these calls and how on every occasion the factor eventually agreed to send some of the estate workers over for a few hours. He though could not recall many times when the LFS workers ended up doing the job!

LFS moved into new buildings in the early 1970s where the chandlery today sits, and numerous sheds were built alongside a large parking area behind "the ranch" for boat crews' cars.

One of the major challenges at the time was that the fish were being landed and sold on the harbour and there were increasing calls for a covered fish market.

Fish sales outdoors (credit: John C. MacLeod)

Before the decade was out another harbour extension added the finger jetty with the covered fish market which provided a considerably drier experience in the Winter (and often Summer) months.

The second larger ice plant was another notable cause for celebration as a newspaper clipping highlights below:

Celebrating the new ice plant (credit: Wilma MacAskill)

Lochinver pier 1984 (credit: Gwen Richards)

Covered fish market (credit: Roy MacLeod)

Many of the crews from the East coast were keen golfers and would set off early on a Sunday to get in a round of golf together before continuing the drive through to the West coast. One harbour worker whose duties included filling those cars with fuel noted that cars left parked at the back of the harbour often with keys in the ignitions and three or four full sets of clubs in the back. It would have been a thief's dream.

During the 1970s, the business also changed somewhat with lorries purchased and the company taking on the running of the fish market as well as investing in new boats and taking on the management of others.

Hector MacKenzie recalled the busiest night he worked on at the harbour in the mid 1970s when 24 lorries were filled with fish. This of course, was before the days of forklift trucks, so boxes were dragged across the market with a hook either side (it helped if the floor was wet) and if necessary piled on to a four wheeled trolley to get them over to the lorry and hand lifted seven boxes high on the back of the truck before being secured.

Boxes were wooden and prone to fail, so it was not unusual to lift a box on to the top level (always the top one) and have the bottom give way and the entire eight stone load fall out and require re-packing.

Trolley loaded with boxes (credit: John C. MacLeod)

By the end of the 1970s, Lochinver Fish Selling had seven lorries of its own - although many of the buyers had their own transport also.

This was one of the strengths of the business, but potentially also a weakness. If a lorry broke down or there was a particularly large landing, the biggest challenge was getting enough transport into the port to handle the number of fish going out.

Harbour staff joked that they always knew when there was a big load coming in as most of the senior guys and particularly George Mackay would be almost impossible to get hold of.

George spent the early part of most afternoons on the radio to various boats to determine if they would be landing that evening – most boats were at sea for two or three days to ensure they landed as fresh a catch as possible whilst also making sure they maximised fishing time. He would take that information and call buyers and transporters with an update on the expected market size, and everyone knew when to expect a busy night either because he had called them directly or because he was spending so much time on the phone calling hauliers all around the North trying to source additional transport to get the expected number of fish out of the port.

One harbour worker recalled the origins of what is now a major haulier. Two brothers, one of which was a chef to trade were amongst the first to see a demand for prawns – fuelled perhaps by his own trade. The brothers though had between them only the one "clapped out" car and driving through to the West coast really wasn't much of an option for them, so arranged initially for a Lochinver buyer to bring two boxes – one of prawns and one mixed fish – every week on their usual load and met him at the Struie junction. It wasn't long before the word got out about the quality of their produce and it wasn't too long before the business grew to the point where they bought a fishmongers and a van that they used to come across west themselves. The story goes that one of the ties they built in Lochinver also suggested that they bought a small stretch of river so they could also purchase locally "sourced" salmon and sell it as caught on their own river. It is unlikely that this happened, but it highlights the entrepreneurial spirit on the harbour at the time and the part the port played in the creating of what is now a major haulage business.

For many, their first job as a teenager involved gathering old fish boxes from the shore to be mended and re-used. Unfortunately, a broken fish box was of no use on board a boat and many – rather than take them back for repair – simply chucked them over the side. It was not unusual for a trolley to work its way along the length of the village collecting and returning full of battered and sea-worn boxes.

Fish boxes were made and repaired in a large shed at the entrance to the harbour and it became virtually a rite of passage for many local teenagers to spend their Summer holidays working on the boxes under the watchful eye of Magnus Mackay. Mag was the eldest MacKay brother. He never tired of reminding his brother or anyone else of this. He suffered from some chronic health issues but is more remembered for both a wicked temper and a wicked sense of humour – there would be few young lads up to high jinx who would not remember a hammer crashing into a box next to them as Mag called for order or the many laughs to be had working on the boxes.

Perhaps the one thing most people remember Mag for was his description of a local boat where the owner enjoyed a drink. The boats all had a unique number showing the port of registration "That boat should have been registered as VAT69" (a well-known brand of whisky).

Mag particularly enjoyed nothing more than winding his brother up, so when an alternative fish market appeared courtesy of the box shed, you don't need to imagine the hand rubbing and wide grin as he endorsed the project.

Alternative fish market (credit: Nick Groves)

A crucial part of the appeal at Lochinver was the menial jobs done by the harbour staff to help those on the fishing boats concentrate on their job. Crew worked hard all week and enjoyed their precious time off at the weekends. The last things they wanted was to spend that time shopping for the following weeks meals and even worse arriving back to a cold damp boat. Knowing that they could arrive in Lochinver with the week's supplies purchased accounts already booked to the boat, goods packed away, the boat fully fuelled, iced, the engine already running, and the boat warm was both welcomed and acknowledged as a level of service they would not receive in every port.

Investment brought investment and there are fond memories of the Kelvin Hughes (Decca) offices where navigation equipment was maintained – and "any electrical issues could be dealt with". The main piece of equipment was the "Decca navigator" which at the time competed with Global Positioning System (GPS) as the primary system for locating vessels. Decca was preferred by fishermen as the system of

3 lanes (purple, red and green) which crossed one another to provide a fixed point of reference was believed to be by far the most accurate. Ultimately it was unable to compete with cheaper alternatives.

One ex-fisher recalled a particularly challenging call for the Decca engineer. The crew in question had been on a wild weekend and when Monday morning came, the skipper was keen to get back to sea. The crew were, to a man, less so and one nameless character was clearly in need of a little bit more "recovery time".

The skipper was insistent – there were bills to pay – and he went below decks to start the engine. As he went below, one of the crew went up on top of the wheelhouse and popped a nail through the Decca Navigator cable.

With no navigation, the craft was unable to get much further than halfway out Lochinver bay before turning back to call the engineer. Repair was swift, once he arrived, but long enough to ensure the hangover was cured.

In time LFS became a one stop shop covering harbour management, ice and fuel supply, fish market management, buying, selling and shipping of fish as well as the supply of chandlery needs and shopping for the boats.

In the heyday of the company the level of service they provided for fishermen was quite exceptional. It was far from unknown for harbour workers to get a phone call at 1am to sort something. The something could be anything from a mechanical issue, a need for more ice to "I've crashed my car, can you get me a lift and organise a breakdown truck to recover it in the morning".

Once or twice the lift would be given by the harbour team and could be for a considerable distance. One even recalled being asked to make sure he returned the car to the harbour to hide the evidence that the driver - who was in no fit state to drive - had ever been in it.

In the early 1970s a boat building factory was erected at Baddidarroch and by 1977 there was also a factory at the top of the Glac Mhor hill packing fish for mail order.

Shellfish processing (credit: Highland Focus)

In the 1980s on the same site a larger business specialising in shellfish for the continental market and later at the employing over a dozen folk.

By 1986, the LFS, now owned by Salvesen, business had 35 full time employees, shares in 9 fishing boats and management responsibility for 14 others.

Superstition

Perhaps more than in any other community, the degree to which superstitions dominated the community is remarkable. Even amongst those who claimed to have no superstition at all, if you were to ask an innocent question like "did you ever have a woman on the crew?" the response would more likely to be "I have never had a woman on the boat – that's bad luck" than a simple "no".

Virtually every former (and current) fisher noted one or more superstitions they either kept to themselves or knew of someone they had worked with who did. Some are curious, some are downright strange, but it is perhaps a measure of the dangers at sea that small charms or habits were such a prominent part of their story.

Women, ministers and taxmen were all mentioned regularly in interviews as folk who would not be allowed to set foot on a boat – the last one was in all likelyhood, tongue in cheek. Ministers would visit the harbour but would rarely set foot on a boat and would never do so without invitation.

The exception to this was the superintendent of the Royal National Mission to Deep Sea Fishermen ("the mission"). The "Mission man" (it was always a man) was held in high esteem by the crews – even those who were not religious and were always more than happy to provide an ear for any troubles and sometimes more importantly, a cup of tea.

Mission building (credit: John C. MacLeod)

Swans were always seen as an unlucky bird for fishers and in many cases this extended beyond the bird to a brand of matches which featured a bird on the box.

One of the services offered by LFS was to pick up the weekly supplies for the boats and staff noted when picking up the order that unlucky "Swan Vestas" matches would never be supplied to the boats. Others would turn for home at the mention of pigs ("Cal Irn" or curly tails) or Salmon ("Sannies" or "red fish") whilst at sea.

One local fisher recalled that as a young man he brought a salmon sandwich on board for lunch and stopped for a bite to eat while the net was out trawling. He would never forget the mouthful he received from the skipper for bringing red fish on board and being told never to mention the contents to the rest of the crew. However, when the net came in, it was a massive haul and with no more word said, he noted that there was a tin of salmon for him in the next weeks supplies on the boat.

Some skippers, such as Murdo King would, if they were not as sea themselves, rail at anyone who dared to whistle in the house when boats were at sea. Certainly not on the boat itself – the reasoning being that whistling was "calling the wind".

There was a lady in Lochinver, who was said to be a buidseach (pronounced Bushnak and meaning a witch or a curse) by local fishermen. Although she never actively cursed any of them - at least to the best of my knowledge - if she was spotted by fishermen on their way to the boat, they knew beyond all doubt that the fishing would be poor, or their gear would be torn. So, knowing the inevitable, they would turn round and go home.

Although this sounds a minor tale, the consequences are worth thinking about – a boat would have a crew of three, four or five men and their wage was a share of the catch. No going to sea meant no catch and no earnings. When you consider that the weather could cause enough days to be lost it was no small sacrifice for an entire crew to make just because they saw this one lady. The skipper in question was unbending in his belief that the buidseach was real.

Other superstitions were more fatalistic. Many fishermen never learned to swim believing that "If the good lord wants to take me, why would I fight it". There are stories among the older fishers of their predecessors putting tackets (metal grips) in their boots so that if they went overboard, they would go down quicker.

One skipper shared that belief in not fighting fate by learning to swim though he was happy to relate the tale of a crewman who went over the side and was saved after being pulled from the water. In another tale recalled by a local skipper:

Back when I was just a deckhand on another boat, there was a young lad in his first week at the sea given the task of hooking the dahn buoy for the net. The normal practice was to catch the rope with a "creeper"

– a large four-pronged metal hook with a rope attached which would be thrown and used to snag the dahn rope and pull it in. On this occasion, whether through lack of explanation or foolhardiness, the lad reached to grab it by hand and a combination of the weight of the buoy and pole with the run of the swell meant that rather then the lad lifting the dahn, the reverse happened, and he was pulled into the water clinging desperately to the pole.

Normally the boat would be close to stopped at this point, but there was always movement in the water and momentum was taking them apart. It took a quick-thinking crewman to throw a lifebelt where it was needed and get the lad back on deck.

As for superstition, the storyteller noted that "our wee offering to the sea must have been appreciated, the catch was pretty decent when it finally came in".

Some were more sanguine in their thoughts "I don't have time for any superstition, fishermen understand the weather, the wind, the flights and calls of birds and the tides but they have never understood what was under them in the water, and many superstitions are based on experience of what had worked previously or had not" – John Thompson.

In a very few words, Johnnie outlined so many of the skills of the fisher – knowing that birds might indicate fish below the surface, when the right tide might move a shoal higher or lower in the water when the conditions are right to lay a net and bring home a catch.

His choice of words says so much about fishermen – he was a "forager of the seas" rather than a mere fisher and much of our conversation talked about the fishing "family" how some may have had superstitions and foibles, but that they saw themselves as all in it together.

There was one tradition which trod the line between superstition and religion – respect for the "Sabbath". Whether it was a legal requirement or an unwritten law, no boat would set sail on a Sunday. It was not unknown though for an engine to be running at 11:59pm and a crewman holding a rope on the pier to cast off when the second hand finally reached the top of the dial – particularly on those weekends after a fortnight of bad weather.

One recently retired fisher recounted the day he first set sail on the sabbath. "It was in the Winter after weeks of horrendous weather – just awful, six days of the week, but as fate would have it, we'd enjoyed a couple of lovely Sundays when I could have been at sea.

So, I decided in the week after the wind came up on the Monday morning again, that if the weather was good on the Sunday, I would take a chance. I cannot tell you how nervous I was, wondering whether I would be struck down or whether anyone in the village would talk to me ever again. I deliberately set off at about 4am when nobody would be awake and went out the bay in pitch darkness checking all the way out for someone's light to come on, but none did and I'm not sure if anyone even noticed my boat wasn't there in the morning. In the end, it was no different to any other day at sea. Neither a bad nor a good days fishing, but enough to give me the confidence to go again.

Superstition played it's part in local events as well. The Highland games are possibly the biggest annual event in Assynt and it has been a long-held tradition that the honorary "chieftain" of the games will arrive on his "barge" for the day – which tradition always had as a fishing boat, though in recent years, the local RNLI lifeboat has taken on this function.

It was an honour for the skipper to have their boat chosen as the chieftain's barge and an effort was always made to make sure the craft was scrubbed and decorated with flags to make it look the part (for what was essentially a short trip out the bay and back to allow the chieftain to arrive in style.

A decorated barge (Atlantis INS73) arriving at the pier (credit: Alan MacLeod)

However, the chieftain would be accompanied by a retinue of friends and family for the trip and there were a few skippers who frowned on the idea of having a woman on board the boat. Sadly, this meant that on occasion the barge originally selected would have to be substituted for one with a less superstitious skipper.

Not all shared this opinion of course and it was not unknown for a local lass to pop down on one of the boats to share an evening meal – particularly if they sensed a more ongoing relationship might result. One lady joked when asked about how she met her husband – "I was fishing, just like the menfolk. Some of us though, did our fishing by dangling our legs as bait over the harbour wall".

Characters and memories

The harbour was noted for a hard work hard play ethos which gave rise to some interesting characters and stories.

A harbour worker noted that one (nameless) employee used to take his lunchbreak at the same time every day almost as if he were clockwatching, but it was known that he did not wear a wristwatch. A curious colleague eventually got to asking him how with no clock in sight and no wristwatch, he knew when to stop for lunch at the same time each day. Simple was the reply, you just pop back here tomorrow at five minutes before one and I would be happy to show you. The following day, he duly turned up and arrived just in time for the man to nod in the direction of another man from the harbour office heading for the pub door as he did every day at the same time.

Humour was also a key part of life on the harbour side and a skipper recalled his father-in-law spotting something on a coil of rope. He was pretty sure it was just a piece of seaweed, but looked more suspicious, so he had no issue loudly exclaiming "Davie, where did you do the business when you did your business?" much to the embarrassment of the poor man standing closest to the rope in question.

In another incident a local driver well known for his foul language as well as sharp wit was berated by a local lady for something and he replied with "and why would I listen to you? You're just a crabbit f****** b****". The lady in question was so incensed to be spoken to in that manner that she replied without thinking "I am not a crabbit f***** anything and ohh you're the first person to make me swear in many's a year" – much to the amusement of her tormentor and everyone on the harbour.

For some reason harbours attract the strangest and most interesting of characters. One of those was called "Sputnik" – he had predicted space exploration some time before the Russians first put a craft into space and was forever seeing flashing lights in the sky. Hugh soon got the nickname sputnik and in fairness most local folk thought him stone mad until a visiting student got into a conversation with him at a dance and then spent much of the following day trying to find out who he was. As it happened, he was a genuine rocket scientist in his final year of study and noted that Hugh had given him a better explanation of the module he was working on than his professor at the university was ever able to, but that he also had a feeling that his knowledge of Chemistry was mostly on how to make mind altering concoctions. Where he got his knowledge from is anyone's guess, but his reputation improved considerably as a result.

The same man worked in the kitchen of the Culag hotel and swore blind he could tell the difference between a seine net caught fish and a trawl caught fish – he was invariably right.

Despite it being a place of work, the harbour was always buzzing with visitors and local children taking an interest in what was going on.

John C. MacLeod recalled one day when his brother and another lad were playing on a boat. The crew would have been away home for the weekend and as kids do, the two lads were throwing the creeper (hook for grabbing the bouy when seine netting) in the water and hauling it back in by the rope.

Of course, the inevitable happened and one of them didn't hold the rope tightly enough as the creeper was thrown. It disappeared into the water and the boys disappeared just as quickly as the rapidly sinking metal hook.

Unfortunately, no-one mentioned this to the skipper who set of to sea when they returned after the weekend.

On spotting a child (John) on the harbour on his way in shouted: "Hail sair a day wi nae creeper an having to use a boat hook gather the dahn".

John noted that despite having nothing to do with losing the creeper, he feared the skipper (the man in question was notably one of the easiest going men in the port) until the day he retired.

Work hard and play hard, particularly in the 1970s, was part of the culture, if not always a great combination. Perhaps best illustrated by an image that would put most health and safety executives into palpitations.

Fortitude being lifted by crane (credit: John C. MacLeod)

One lorry driver was notorious for setting off after a full day of work elsewhere and when he was clearly in need of a lie down.

One interviewee recalled as a youngster, getting a lift with another driver over to the east coast. Seeing a glow in the distance near Altguish, they natural slowed down and discovered it was a Lochinver Fish Selling lorry with its engine running, stationary in a passing place next to the loch with the driver sound asleep at the wheel.

The driver he had hitched a ride with warned him to keep his distance as the driver "was prone to lash out when disturbed".

He then returned to his own lorry and produced a broom from behind his seat and prodded the sleeping driver awake. Sure enough, the first reaction was for the fists to fly – fortunately, doing no significant damage to the broom.

Without a word, the door was slammed shut and the driver in question took off like a hare and was next seen at their destination, again asleep in front of the wheel having already delivered his load.

Until the mid 1970s many of the roads were single track with passing places and with drivers mostly working late at night the roads were not always at their best. Drivers recalled that it was always their decision as to whether it was safe to travel or not and one recalled a snowy night where he felt that the buyers had made it safely up from the East coast, so it would be safe enough for him to head off in the other direction. He recalled a virtual white-out in the village and skidding to a stop on the middle of the village where "Big MacKay" (George) stood in the middle of the road with his arms folded and demanding to know if he really wanted to put his life at risk for a load of fish. The driver recalled that he took some convincing that his own profits on the run was a fair price to pay for risking one of his drivers lives. The man proudly noted being told that it was on his head and he delivered the load.

The drivers of course were all too aware that the risks they took on the roads were minimal when compared to the risks at sea:

One local fisher recalling his time on board the Zenith with the trawl net out receiving a radio message that there was weather coming in from the South West. The weather forecasts in those days were decent, but sometimes a squall just came up out of nowhere and the first notice you might get would be a radio call from someone else already experiencing it.

The boat was outside of the three-mile limit and there was no way they'd be able to get the net in and get back to the harbour before they took a battering, so the decision was made to head for the other side of Stoer head and hopefully get some shelter in the lee of the hills.

Of course, this meant hauling the net in first because you could make no speed with that dragging behind you.

He recalled a comic mix of the wind and waves rising as they steamed in the general direction of Stoer head hauling the net in as they went and hoping to get everything stowed before the storm hit properly. It was a rough time before they were able to make proper progress and in the end most of the catch was thrown below without even sorting.

As they rounded Stoer head, it became apparent that they were not the only ones with the same thought and finding a spot that was out of the worst of the wind and still away from the rocks enough to be safe wasn't going to be possible. Some more frantic radio calls and the decision was made to tie up with other boats tight enough that they wouldn't smash each other to bits in the most sheltered spot. Not the most comfortable of nights was the stoic description.

MV Zenith (credit: John C. MacLeod)

Lorries and buggies although technically company vehicles, were sometimes used for personal use.

One harbour worker recalled a night in the local bar, which for him was a rarity, but on this occasion, he had enjoyed a few and when the evening ended he decided to take the LFS buggy rather than walk home to Stoer. He had drunk enough to know he shouldn't be driving, but also enough to take the chance and when he was on the straight at Loch an Ordain he saw some headlights in the distance behind him.

There would not have been many cars on the road at that time and fearing it was the police combined with knowing he had a few made him panic. So, he turned off the lights and drove the buggy up the unsurfaced peat road before taking off on foot over the hills – to this day he has no idea who was behind him.

One of the original LFS lorries (credit: John C. MacLeod)

Changing LFS Lorry liveries (credit: Murdo Aird)

One lorry driver would often use "his" truck to nip down to Inverness for an antiques auction and Ian Nurse recalled when he was still a teenager, one Friday being asked if he would help on his day off as the man was planning to purchase something, he would need help to load.

The driver was successful in his bidding and got the item at a very good price – so good, that he felt the need of a dram to celebrate.

Ian recalled sitting in the cab for some time at the tail end of a busy Friday afternoon as the whole of academy street being brought to a halt by the lorry being reversed slowly by an inebriated driver into a loading bay at the auction house before a stand-up shouting match with a traffic warden slowed procedures even more.

He did not recall the item purchased but could not forget the conversation on the Monday morning when word got back that an LFS livery lorry caused a major traffic incident in Inverness.

The incident was smoothed over quickly he recalled by the fast-thinking driver. LFS were of course a fish haulier, but there was a significant part of the business dedicated to bringing loads back to Lochinver. Whether it was car parts from MacRae and Dick for garages across the region, animal feed or chandlery items coming into the shop, they would normally arrive on a returning lorry – the auction incident was explained away as just another stop on a journey home.

One employee noted that the police rarely stopped lorry drivers, except when hoping for a fry and recalled when he was 17 being asked to take a lorry across to the East coast after a driver had taken ill. He pointed out that although he could drive, he didn't have an HGV licence (and couldn't apply for one until he was 21) but was offered £60 cash for taking the trip and told if the police stopped him, that there was a loose box at the back of the truck and just offer them a fry of fish.

As fate would have it, he was stopped just outside Beauly and the officer said, "You're not the usual driver". Fearing he was about to be arrested, he blurted out "No, he's taken ill, but he asked me to make sure I brought some fish for you" hopped out of the cab and pulled down the box, which promptly disappeared into the boot of the police car and they drove off "without even checking my name, much less my licence". He did note though that he was berated on his return as a "fry" was not normally an entire box.

One driver was known for his quick wit and foul language and stories of his comments came thick and fast – unfortunately most are unprintable. Amongst the few (barely) printable was his description of a rather gangly harbour worker as 'the only man who could put an arm round your shoulder and scratch your backside at the same time".

One character locally arrived as a fisherman, but after leaving the boat he had arrived with, remained as a feature on the harbour, employed on a cash basis by a variety of skippers for odd jobs – whether that being collecting their order from the shop and laying it by on the boat, starting the engines before the crew arrived or on some of the older boats lighting the coal fire cooker on the boat so it was ready to go and of course taking the boats round to make sure they were fuelled and iced in readiness for the crews – though it was noted that he never possessed a skippers ticket so it was fortunate there was never an accident, as he would have had no legal right to do so.

At times he slept on an old leisure boat propped up at the back of the harbour – something picked up by the owner when he returned after a winter away to find it awash with cigarette butts. He was also in the summer months camping in Culag woods and sometimes at weekends sleeping on boats at the harbour if they were unlocked. Eventually LFS provided him with a caravan to live in.

Fishermen often referred to themselves as hunters of the sea and they would guard a good spot or piece of migratory knowledge jealously. One skipper was known on the harbour for unfailingly landing a large haul of halibut every year around the same time. He would never reveal where he caught them.

One day as he was walking across the harbour he was asked if he was off to get that first load of halibut and it was as if a chill came over the whole harbour as he stopped, turned on the spot and demanded "Fit de ye ken aboot halibuts".

There was a spluttered reply of "well isn't this when you always land a catch of halibut? It's usually the biggest landing of the year".

Again, there was a glare in the skippers' eye as he demanded to know who was keeping tabs on when he landed what.

The reason the man knew – and indeed everyone on the harbour knew was that this same skipper had every year for the previous decade brought in a huge catch of halibut on the Thursday before the first week of Wimbledon tennis. This was just one example of the way fishermen worked - they had spots they knew would produce results and they knew when they would do so. Even to the point where everyone knew what they would bring home in a given week.

Hunters of the sea often kept meticulous records. One widow recalled destroying dozens of books after her husband's loss – something she now regrets – meticulously detailing what had been caught where, which species appeared where in what months, what weather, which tides, where there were rocks on the bottom, currents, tides. "they weren't quite diaries, as there were no personal thoughts, just scribbled notes going back decades".

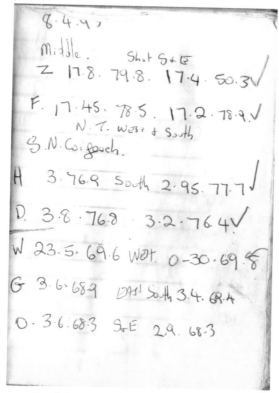

One fishers meticulous notes from April 1995

The drivers who delivered their catches are also a rich source of memories. In the 1970s one had a side-line as a coal merchant – which was a good business if he remembered to deliver the coal, but he noted himself that sometimes he would forget and tell customers to just help themselves and "settle up" later.

He was a huge character and subject to a few good tales:

On one occasion with a newly acquired lorry (purchased from LFS and repainted) he managed to run into a herd of cows near Rogart. Sadly not a tale that has grown legs with telling - hitting one would have been tragedy enough, but it was an entire herd on the road. Standing in the mess of perhaps a dozen carcasses he was being berated by the owner when the police arrived and the lady in question was particularly upset at the loss of one animal – "My pet cow, you've killed my pet cow".

It is said that the police report quoted his reply: "B****r your cow, you've killed my pet lorry".

One day the same gentleman was delivering coal to a boat in the harbour (many of the older boats had coal fired ovens in the galley for heat and cooking).

The boat in question was the last in a line of five tied to the harbour when the driver and two helpers arrived just before 11am and they decided that as it was a hot day it might be a good idea that as the bar had just opened to stop in for a quick drink before they got on with the thirsty work of loading coal on to and across a line of boats.

This might have been a good plan if it wasn't that they had arrived at high tide and by the time they had enjoyed a (none too) swift drink, the tide was at its lowest ebb and the boats were now around 20 feet lower than the side of the harbour.

It is said, that the bar emptied watching the three men trying to lower heavy sacks of coal without spilling them before they could get them on to the boat they needed.

There were many dangers associated with fishing from hitting the rocks to scooping up something you shouldn't. One local trawlerman was stopped by the fisheries protection vessel (the police of the sea) for fishing inside the three-mile limit. His defence stood – he had caught a large boulder and it was too heavy to haul it on to the deck and all they were able to do was pull it behind the boat until they got into the shallow waters of the harbour where they could roll it out a low tide – he noted that it took a very close inspection and visual proof of the rock in the net before he was let off.

The harbour also supported mechanics, divers, welders, electricians, and numerous other trades providing services for the fishing industry. It would never have survived without the – often out of hours - efforts of so many great people.

Harbour work often took place at odd hours – if something was needed for one of the boats, you just got up and did it, but one worker who was working the wee small hours one night spotted a very experienced skipper "mooching around the fish box shed and removing a number of bits of wood".

He said nothing and didn't even make his presence known but noted that the mans boat wasn't in its normal berth that night – instead tucked right up next to the Culag park where the tide would drop enough to allow a man to go down on the waterline. A little later in the evening, he heard hammering.

The boat in question was gone the following morning and unusually didn't appear back in Lochinver for a couple of weeks.

It took some serious prying with a crewmember before the story made sense. It appeared that the skipper in question had caught a rock near Stoer Head and the boat was holed and taking in water. The crewman admitted that it had been a worrying steam back to the harbour with a deeply embarrassed man at the wheel.

They laid up for the night and by morning a few additional planks were nailed inside and out and sealed with a chemical metal bond and they set off for the East coast boatyard for more permanent repairs – hopefully with no-one on the West coast port knowing where or why they were gone. To this day, our storyteller doubts the skipper knew he had been found out.

A character in the village was Jimmy Young who was never a man to miss a business opportunity. When the Kylesku ferry was replaced in the late 1960s Jimmy purchased the old one – the "Mamore". The craft had been designed to transport cars from one side of a sheltered loch to the other, so was far from the ideal craft to fish on the open seas and this may have been discovered on the journey from Kylesku round to Lochinver, as it is rumoured to have only gone out once after that – spending many years after berthed on the roadside next to Culag bridge.

The one trip it did go out was notable though - fishing herring with a ring net in Lochinver bay being serenaded as the net was laid by crewmember Ian (Jeemak) MacLeod in the middle of the deck playing on the accordion, before he put it down to help haul in the catch. They were fishing close enough to the harbour that they could be heard from the shore and drew quite a crowd.

Angus MacLeod was bald - the mop head is indeed a mop (credit: Alex McBain)

Unlike cars, fishing boats were hand and custom built. A trained local eye could pick out who was coming in the bay just from the shape. One or two had distinctive colours and some of the older ones even had portholes along the side. One such craft used to be visited regularly by a member of staff from the Culag hotel who would bring the skipper his dinner most nights. It was during one of these "dining" visits that another craft arrived at the harbour and the skipper happened, as they cruised past to see through the porthole that there were two individuals in a state of undress. Now, fishermen are a discreet and respectful bunch, so nothing was made of the incident – except to inform the crew that they would have a cuppa before landing and asking one of the younger deckhands to pop over on to the boat in question to borrow a tin of milk for their tea – the cuppa, already with milk in it was handed over as he returned flushed with embarrassment.

Something many recall fondly in the village is that there was always someone who would offer a fry of fish if you needed one – fish were sold by the box and there was often a part box left over which would be happily shared, but one skipper recalled being berated by the local fishmonger for giving away his business. After some negotiation it was agreed that fishers would leave any fry beside the lifeboat donation box where there was a sign saying these were there for anyone willing to leave a donation. This solution worked very well for all parties.

Lifeboat box - often with a box of fish below (credit: Alan MacLeod)

The fish themselves are part of the history – many older fishers recall that prawns (langoustines) and lobsters would occasionally come up in the net, especially in the early days of trawl netting and not having a market for them meant they were thrown over the side. More than one noted that if only they had known how delicious they were, they would have been kept for the crew. Once a market developed in the early 1970s, these became highly prized.

During the 1970s a market opened for monkfish as a cheaper alternative to prawns as chefs discovered that slices of the tail both looked and tasted similar to the prawn. In fact, this market opening meant the price for prawns went down and led to a protest in Lochinver in 1975 when some creel fishers gave away prawns for free in the middle of the village (after first making sure the press were in attendance).

Prawn protest (credit: John C. MacLeod)

The similarity in taste meant that chefs could offer a cheaper alternative to the popular scampi dish – of course never telling the customer what they were eating. One fisherman's wife recalled the disgust in her husband's voice one afternoon when he ordered "Scampi" in an Inverness restaurant and after the first bite realised, he had been served the cheaper Monks tails – the dish was returned to the kitchen. Strangely those same monk tails now sell for about double the price that prawns now make.

Sorting prawns (credit: John C. MacLeod)

In a similar tale a lad who worked on a fishing boat each summer during his college course had in his first summer of working been told to throw dogfish over the side – they were just tasteless scavengers.

On his first trip the following summer, he repeated the process of the previous year, only to be asked what on earth he was up to before being told "The English eat them".

It seemed that some buyers from down south found the emerging market prices for them cheaper in the West Highlands. As soon as there was a market, they became a valued catch.

It was not that the market had opened that stuck with him, it was the way it was described, and he noted that he still cannot pass a fishmonger selling "rock salmon", "rock" or "huss" (all terms used for dogfish) without a wry smile for that strange alien people who once consumed them.

One task every local skipper hated but did for the community was the transport of livestock. Centuries old tradition meant that animals were kept close to home over the winter months, but in the summer when things were growing, they had traditionally been moved away from the crops to higher pastures. It was common to put the animals on to an island over the summer months to keep them away from whatever was growing on the croft. Local fishermen would provide the transport and right through the 1970s there was a regular run out to Soyea in the Spring and a collection early Autumn. Although happy to help, it was never easy to get sheep on and off the boat at either end and the mess they left on the deck took days to clean properly – a skipper's wife noted "he reckoned the landing on an island with no pier and at best a dodgy beach was the best part of it – it meant the sheep were off the boat".

Boats were typically fishing two or three-day stints balancing the maximum time at sea with bringing the fish to port as fresh as possible. Although they would land and be off back to sea at the first opportunity, the return to port was also one of the few opportunities for catching up on sleep.

Generally, there would be little fishing done over the weekends and as boats were rarely locked and anyone could start an engine (there was no key) it wasn't unknown for a boat to go missing on a Friday or Saturday night as the bar emptied and word of a party planned at the White Shore or Achmelvich got around. What better way to get there than on a boat?

Several interviewees had memories of revellers swimming to shore and music blasting a few yards out the bay on a "party craft". Normally the skippers would not be aware their boats had been taken and they would be safely back on their berth the following morning.

On several occasions, the boat spent longer than intended at Achmelvich due to the party being on the night of a high "Spring tide" and the boat being left stranded on the tides fall.

Tragedy and loss

Not one interview was conducted where tragedy at sea or in the harbour didn't raise a spectre of the past. Fishing is known to be amongst the most dangerous of professions. Between long hours, fragmented sleep (particularly whilst seine netting where if the fishing was good, fishers might work 18 of 24 hours with the 6 remaining hours being made up of three short naps) and of course weather and rocks, fishing was never a career choice for the risk adverse. Losses were rarely frequent, but they were ever present, and it is perhaps only in memory that the scale of loss becomes apparent.

In the words of Duncan King at the height of the fishing boom "There will be a time when there will be no fish left in the Minch. This just can't go on: We'll have to go back to line and creel fishing again… It will have to be the Atlantic next and the boats will have to be big enough and safe enough to go there… taking chances – trying to make ends meet: Out boats just aren't big enough". A prophesy that Nostradumus would have been proud of.

Duncan marvelled in the 1970s at boats like the Arctic Riever with it's covered deck and safety features. He knew all to well the risks that fishers took on a daily basis.

For every loss of course, there would be many near misses and thankfully the services of the coastguard and the Royal National Lifeboat Institute (RNLI) helped prevent many tragedies.

The lifeboats have been a vital service in the parish since 1967. From an original volunteer crew (as today, often fishermen themselves) it was not unknown for the departing lifeboat to pull alongside an incoming trawler for long enough to allow crew to hop from one to the other to ensure a full crew were present for the call.

Lochinvers first lifeboat the Dunleary (credit: Jean McBain)

One fisherman's widow admitted she was nervous every time her husband and sons went to sea, but she was never as nervous as when her husband went out on the lifeboat.

The first boat in Lochinver didn't have the anti-rolling technology they have now, or even a covered deck for that matter. It was a rule of thumb that the lifeboat was only ever called out in bad weather. A wise skipper she recounted would listen to the fishing forecast and read the weather like a good book. If the weather wasn't in it, they would never leave the harbour, but the lifeboat was usually called out when someone made the wrong judgement on conditions.

She recalled one wild night when they were at a dance in the village hall. It was one of those nights when even the lifeboat crew felt no-one would be daft enough to be at sea, so felt able to relax for the evening. Sure enough though, three flares went off. She recalled that the lifeboat muster signal was always three – although she couldn't be sure, she thought there was a different number for coastguard.

It struck her memory as the band had just struck up "Dark Island" and being such a sad song, it left her chilled when the flares went off.

The crew learned that a small blue boat had been spotted struggling in heavy seas near Achiltibuie and the crew went to look for it. They searched all night in appalling conditions and wives and partners ashore spent a sleepless night wondering if they or the wee boat would ever make it back.

On the following morning though as the sun rose, the lifeboat made its way back to the harbour with no sign of the craft they were looking for.

Several hours later she recalled a knock at the front door and a man she didn't know asking to speak to her husband, to whom he presented with a bottle of whisky.

It turned out that he was the owner of the small green (not blue) boat and had landed safely in Lochinver just as the lifeboat was heading out the bay. Being the wrong colour of boat, no-one had batted an eye as they passed one another.

Angus Scott, William "Pomp" MacLeod and, Graham Anderson: (credit: Katherine Anderson)

Older fishers note that the professionalism has grown year on year as more training is provided and some full-time crew being able to man faster and more capable craft.

There are many skippers who have suffered engine failure, or a rope caught in the propellor and can thank the RNLI for a tow back to the safety of the harbour.

Lochinvers first 'new' lifeboat (previously the boat had come from somewhere else) the George Urie Scott from 1969-1978 (credit: Katherine Anderson)

A dedication service on board the Ramsey Dyce (credit: Katherine Anderson) Sadly not every life could be saved and there were some tragic losses also.

Perhaps one of the hardest losses was in the mid 1980s when the Sapphire set sail in weather perhaps that they should not have, but the skipper had treated the crew to tickets for a football match and they were sailing round to the east coast to combine a refit with what they hoped would be a lengthy celebration. Their trip got no further than Stoer Head and unfortunately, it was several days before anyone noticed they were missing - family were waiting for the boat to sail around the North coast and unsure of when they'd left and friends in Lochinver thought they were safely on the other coast. They were not expected back in Lochinver for a week or more and with the wild weather no-one was paying much attention to the coast, so it was some time before a search even began.

MV Sapphire - Lost at Stoer head, 1977 (credit: Malcolm Bangor-Jones Gault)

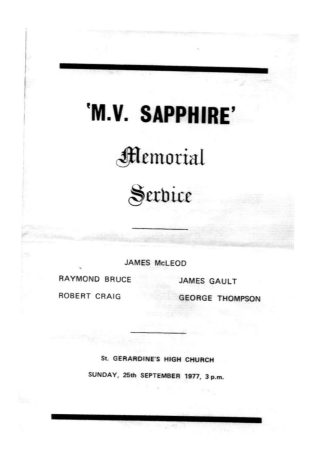

'M.V. SAPPHIRE'

𝔐emorial

𝔖erbice

JAMES McLEOD

RAYMOND BRUCE   JAMES GAULT

ROBERT CRAIG   GEORGE THOMPSON

St. GERARDINE'S HIGH CHURCH

SUNDAY, 25th SEPTEMBER 1977, 3 p.m.

May they rest in peace

It was only a few months later that the Arcadia sunk in very close proximity to the spot the Sapphire was lost. When the Arcadia was lost, the bodies of most of the crew were all recovered from the shoreline fairly quickly but there was no sign of skipper Alec Flett.

Eventually, the search was called off but there was a meeting among the skippers at the harbour where it was agreed that the family needed closure so a team of divers from Stornoway were hired at the skipper's expense to recover his remains.

One of those boats was used to transport the divers back and forth to the dive site and it was some time before they were back to fishing. It would have been a grim but much appreciated task and thankfully successful. The skipper who identified his body for the family described that as the hardest job he had ever done.

This sad tale perhaps highlights more than most the bond that fishermen held with their friends and what were their rivals in trade. They were and remain a community who looked out for one another.

Arcadia crew - some months before her loss (credit: Ian MacLeod)

In a later tragedy, again in foul weather, it is believed that the skipper of the Loch Erisort spotted the lights of a house in Badnaban and mistook it for the harbour – by the time he realised that it was not, they were on the rocks.

The skipper's father was on another boat and on the radio with them at the time, one local recalled he was being led towards the mission for a cup of tea in a state of shock when a newspaper reporter pounced for a quote. The quote she got came from Zandra MacKay who happened to be close by is not printable, but readers can be assured the reporter left very quickly.

Loch Erisort (credit: John C. MacLeod)

As well as boats going down there were individual losses at sea and sadly at the harbour.

On busier nights, six or seven boats could be tied together in a line out from the harbour. A common enough term is to talk about sea legs where the individual gets used to the roll of the boat on the water. It is something that is all too apparent when you first step on a boat from the steadiness of the harbour and when hopping from one boat to another – perhaps with one rising as the other dropped. Even in the relative calm of the harbour, many fishermen have been caught with this over the years and just a single missed step could result in them falling between the boats.

One harbour worker was singled out by several others as having saved numerous fishers from the harbour. Ian "Nurse" MacLeod, when asked about this, with typical understatement, replied "Maybe one or two, but not really". He then went on to describe one man who he watched hop from one boat to another, missed his footing on landing and then fell backwards and hit his head on the rail of the boat he'd just stepped from and ended up face down unconscious in the water. In Ian's words "it was a struggle to get him up the ladder before he woke up". Contemporaries suggested Ian pulled quite a few out of the water.

One of those rescued in this way was a young lad who recalled playing at jumping between the boats as his father chatted to fellow fishermen and missing his footing to go between the boats.

He was soon pulled out but some 50 years later recalls the dressing down he got at home for ruining a new duffel coat.

Usually, these incidents resulted either in the man landing "safely" in the water and climbing out themselves or someone coming to their aid before it was too late, but occasionally the result was a fatality.

Willie Hutchison relayed a tale which he described as something he was ashamed to admit. Some time after he gave up the sea, Willie took over the Culag bar (Wayfairers) and one night whilst on duty behind the bar, a customer spotted a naked man running up and down the pier. Before long everyone was lined up along the window watching what they assumed was someone who was either drunk or mad.

It is perhaps testimony to the many strange events that happened at the harbour that this wasn't seen as anything other than a spectacle.

The naked man eventually ran to the phone box and before long emergency services were on the scene. It turned out that he had been asleep on a boat and had been wakened by a splash. When he went to investigate a crew member was in the water after falling between boats – he had partially stripped to dive in and get the man out and in the struggle had lost what little clothing he had been wearing and his efforts had come to naught as he was unable to get his friend up the ladder and with no one around to hear his calls, he had climbed out and searched along the pier for some help before running to the phone. Sadly, his colleague didn't make it out.

The long hours and tiredness combined with the first building fishers passed as they came of the harbour being the local bar meant that many fishers were all too often tempted in for a swift one while they waited for their pay. With Thursdays and Fridays being "settling up" day, the bar was often packed and even those who were not drinkers would use the bar as a place to pause and reflect with a soft drink or a coffee.

One skipper, who was known for his abstinence, admitted that he occasionally shared one drink – though it was usually a ginger beer - with Ian MacLennan at the end of the week, just to catch up with what had been happening on the land during the week. The long hours at sea meant that fishers rarely had the time to even listen to the news and landing day also became news day.

The bar was as much of a place to catch up as to have a drink and was always busy in the run up to the weekend. This though was always tempered with being keen to get home for some time with the family. One fisher described fishing as a hard job, but nowhere near as hard as bringing up a family single handed while your husband was out at sea and cited his wife as the one who held the family together and enabled him to work the sea.

Perhaps the saddest of stories came from a skipper who fished most of his life from Lochinver, but does not involve the port itself. John Thompson noted that to his knowledge at least half a dozen of his family had been lost to the sea, but the loss that marked him most was a tale his grandfather had told him of two of his own uncles whose boat went down after departing Barra in poor weather. Through a combination of wind and waves, both bodies were recovered but one lies buried in Barra and the other on Lewis.

This perhaps links a couple of common harbour themes. Fishing was a hard life with long hours and back in the day – good rewards.

In one incident, whilst working on the harbour a local skipper heard a splash and ran down the pier to find a harbour worker in the water. He, of course, dived in to help. The man struggled far more than he had expected, pulling away from him on several occasions to get back to the spot he had gone in at. Only once the man had been physically dragged on to the harbour protesting all way, he was coherent enough to exclaim "My half bottle is still in the water".

Sadly, alcohol and tragedy were companions in arms and some fine men were lost after a night on the drink. Memorably, the death of two local men on Assynt games day, was mentioned by many interviewees. They had been enjoying the day and at some point, decided to sit on the stern of the boat one of them worked on for a chat with a carry out.

Several people remember seeing the two of them on the back of the boat, which was not too far from the games field, but no-one heard a splash or saw what happened.

It has been suggested that one toppled over after falling asleep and the other jumped in to help but was cannot be sure other than to note that two bodies were pulled from the harbour that evening.

Another incident resulted in a near miss. A skipper sailing out of Lochinver and on the other side of A' Chleit noticed another craft circling in an ever-widening loop. As time went on, the boat was getting closer to the island and sensing something was amiss, the skipper tried to get hold of them on the radio.

There was no reply and it was becoming clear that in a couple more loops the boat would be on the rocks and they were too far out for the lifeboat to arrive in time.

After consulting with the crew, it was decided that they would have to do something themselves in the meantime.

Edging his own craft alongside as best he could in the swell of the waves, one of the crew leapt from one boat to the other and went inside to investigate.

What he found was a tale in itself – the entire crew sound asleep and the wheel tied with a rope as hard to port as it would go. The skipper having decided that he couldn't stay awake in the state he was in and that if they just circled, what possible harm could they come to?

As it turned out, they were only a few minutes before they found out exactly what harm could come of it. Both boats returned safely to Lochinver harbour tied together.

Sometimes accidents were very close to home (credit: Sandra Callus)

Whilst fishing and drinking were bedfellows, not all fishers drank and it would be far from the truth to suggest that any bar a few losses involved drinking – many of the tragic losses were sober folks.

A tale which does involve alcohol and Assynt, but in an odd way came from Willie Hutchison. In 1953 Willie's father-in-law and uncle bought the Valhalla. They named her after the first craft their own father had worked on and the boat arrived in November of that year. Its arrival coincided with one of the worst winters in living memory and due to the roads being closed and there being no means of getting a catch anywhere other than the village of Lochinver, she was unable to fish for several months until a major effort to re-open the Highlands - operation snowdrift – got things open again.

The Valhalla, is often remembered locally as the craft used to ferry food back and fore to communities around the Stoer peninsula who had no access to any supplies. On one occasion she was even used to transport the local doctor round to Kylesku to deliver a baby. Coincidentally the period was also marked by the arrival of the first helicopter in Assynt – to transport a man with meningitis to the local hospital in Inverness. Many older locals still refer to the rescue helicopter as the "Helico-Peter" after the man in question.

Eventually the roads were opened, the market re-opened and the Valhalla fished very successfully from Lochinver for 20 years before being sold in 1973. The connection of this tale with loss?

As it happens some 10 years later Joan and Willie opened a pub in Inverkirkaig, which of course they called the Valhalla after the boat. Willie had a sign made for the new enterprise and on the day they erected the new sign for the pub, news came through that the old boat had gone down. Continuity is a curious beast.

Some accidents were just that, sober men hard at work who often were lucky to escape with their lives.

Robert "Tubes" MacLaren was standing on a torn net at the back of the boat as they were busy repairing it. The boat struck something, possibly a rock, and Tubes was thrown backwards into the sea. Unfortunately, the current was running against the boat and the first lifebelt thrown to him went awry and they had to circle round before James Buller was able to throw a second which thankfully pulled him out.

It would be remiss to discuss fishing without mention of the Royal National Mission for Deep Sea Fishermen (the mission) which was originally a seaborne service – and a temperance society offering an alternative to drink. The service originally rowed out to boats to offer prayer and supplies, but soon became a physical base with a warm bed and somewhere to relax with a cuppa.

The Mission in Lochinver (now An Cala café) was a welcome place both as a community hub and the draw of hot showers and a warm bed was a strong one. A former superintendent reported that his sermons often drew a larger crowd than the three local churches put together and noted that when he took over and mentioned to three local ladies that it might take a little longer to make them a cup of tea due to the cooker failing in the kitchen it took less than 24 hours before a delegation of local ladies turned up with a bundle of cash to buy a new one. In his words "if there was ever a demonstration of the value of the mission in the community that was it".

The mission was a key part of the harbour life and a key part of the support network at the harbour.

Perhaps not as well-known was how the fishermen supported each other and the families of those affected.

This relationship is evident even today when fishermen pass on, it is amazing how many former colleagues and competitors will travel hundreds of miles to pay their final respects.

For a section on tragedy, it is perhaps best to end on a positive note and one which everyone involved should be justifiably proud of. Skippers rarely talk about it but they donated into weekly into a fund for the families of anyone lost to the sea – there were many and it was their peers, their competitors and ultimately their friends who made sure that their families were supported in their time of most need.

The people and the names

There were of course a lot of names mentioned in compiling this book, but what was remarkable was the memories of bynames and nicknames for people and places that were so ingrained that at times it was challenging to remember the real names of the individuals concerned.

It would be an interesting exercise to find how many outsides of the industry could point out the Achmelvich "haddie hole", the "shambles", the "blue rooms" the "shants", "the wreck" or "the Sticks" off Coigach on a map and it might be challenging also to wonder where some of the names came from.

One fisher recalled the "Airplane shot" – where once a boat had netted debris from a fallen plane. It was at the back of Stoer head.

Others such as the telephone pole shot and the chimney shot were named for landmarks on the shore which told the crew when to drop the net.

As well as locations, the fishers and harbour workers were often given nicknames - which stuck so well that sometimes it was a struggle to remember their real names. Nicknames were given for many reasons, but perhaps most often because across the Highlands many family names were the same (and particularly in fishing families) and nicknames were commonly used to identify individuals.

Many came from their forefathers such as John "Pansy" Stewart on the Ben Loyal, who was named after his father's boat – in the early 1900s there was a fashion for naming craft after flowers. The name was so ingrained that it took a deal of research to find his real name – even a family member when asked his name, replied "He was Pansy".

Ian "Nurse" MacLeod was similarly named for his mothers' profession. There were several Ian MacLeods in the village as Ian "Jeemak", Ian "Strathan" and "Big" Ian would testify. In those cases, his father (James), his birthplace and relative height were the reasons.

Ian "Butch" MacLennnan was named for his first job in Lochinver as a butcher – despite working most of his life on the harbour, he never lost that first name.

Others were named for their place of birth such as Johnnie "Brackloch" MacKenzie or Geordie "Bul Stoer" MacKenzie.

Stewart "Boon" Cowie from the Odyssey was more difficult. Remembered fondly by many interviewees, few knew his given name much less the origins of the nickname. A notoriously shy and quiet man until the first drink when he became everyone's friend. He was also one of the strongest men I can recall – one interviewee recalled enjoying a quiet drink with her dinner on a bar stool and being picked up chair and all by Boon with one hand.

Harper "Happy" Davidson on the Fruitful Bough was a play on his forename rather than any reflection on his temperament though from any conversations I remember with him, he was a cheerful man.

George "Snowy" Smith on the Olive Leaf was named for his light blonde hair and to avoid confusion with his father and "Red" Angus MacLeod for his hair colour also.

John "Pele" Coul because he was a talented footballer in his youth.

Robert "Tubes" MacLaren was in the words of a friend possibly rude, and we will leave it at that. Others were similarly impolite such as the fisherman who was never known to be quiet and referred to as "Gabbie" – neither boat nor real name will be shared to avoid offence.

Jimmy "Fang" Stewart was rarely called by anything other than his byname – it was of course for the single tooth that remained when his false teeth came out.

Jimmy "Fang" Stuart 1981 (credit: Photo: Gwen Richards)

Ronald "Ringo" McBain was my brother and named after the drummer in the Beatles – someone he bore no resemblance to whatsoever but the name stuck.

Donald "Flake" Patience was named according to his own book for telling his crew to flake on the nets as they repaired them (from flake out – to sleep) rather than the more usual lie on them.

Alistair "Para Handy" Campbell, the harbour master was named after a character in a television series of the same name who wore similar headgear.

Ian "Choccy" Anderson was named after the sweets he was always eating as a youngster. When the Marigold landed in Scrabster one night and his brother popped on board and asked to speak to Ian Anderson, no-one on the crew had ever heard him called anything other than choccy and told his poor brother than no-one of that name worked on the boat.

Robert "Rhymer" Young was named for a song about a poet – assume it was a favourite of his.

Of course there were many more memorable characters and nicknames, but hopefully this will give a flavour of the many characters in the fishing community.

Not just Lochinver

Although much of the book has focussed on the larger harbour at Lochinver, there were boats fishing often, but not always, with creels from Badnaban, Drumbeg, Nedd and Kylesku throughout. The harbour at Culkein Stoer also had regular fishing in the early days.

Kylesku, as mentioned previously, was often a safe spot to lay up in a storm and several interviews mentioned a stormy night in the Kylesku hotel, sharing stories with the locally based fishers.

Drifter at Kylesku (credit: John C. MacLeod)

Seaweed

One cannot discuss the Highland clearances without mention of the jobs "created" on the coastal areas for those cleared to them. Often families with no experience of fishing were expected to supplement their income on a poor piece of ground by either fishing or kelp harvesting.

At the time, the kelp was burned and the residue used in a number of products including gunpowder. It is perhaps less well known that the process continued well into the 20th century and as late as the 1980s there were job creation schemes which had people employed to harvest seaweed. Though by this stage, the product was sold by weight and egg wrack (Ascophyllum nodosum) was the preferred crop – as it was heavier.

The employment support often meant that equipment including a boat would be supplied but much of the work was done at low tide on the shore. A short net would be layed on the seaward side of the shore with a rope at either end, leading to the shore and making up three sides of a square.

One member of the crew would cut and wrap weed around the ropes to "bait" the rope and net making the top end thicker. Others would cut all the weed in the centre loose from the rocks. As the tide rose, the seaweed would float, but would not get past the fed ropes which could be pulled together into a rough circle and the weed dragged to a sheltered spot to await collection.

Ring of seaweed (credit: Nick Groves)

The task was not without risk, as one big storm would be enough to encircle several batches of seaweed and cause the entire crop to be lost, Generally for this reason the work was carried out in the summer months. In the words of one seaweed gatherer: "mooching around in the cold winter mud wouldn't be much fun anyway".

A ring of seaweed could contain as much as 12 tonnes of weed and experienced harvesters could on a good day manage up to 4 rings. Harvesters would meet with a craft which gathered from all around the coast and would be paid in cash for their work which took them to many corners of Assynt and beyond.

The Arla lifting egg wrack (credit: Gwen Richards)

Salmon netting at Clachtoll

The Clachtoll salmon station was in use for at least 150 years with the first written record of fishermen living in the bothy coming from the 1851 Census until its eventual closure in mid 1990s

The station was well equipped in comparison to many others along the coast with a drying green, port, ice house as well as the bothy and was generally in operation from April to August.

1970s Clachtoll Salmon Fishers (credit: Alex McBain)

1929 salmon landing records held in the Inchnadamph Old Kirk report a lower-than-average season with over 1100 salmon being caught in the parish – Clachtoll accounted for a significant proportion of those. In its heyday the station reported over 100 fish a day.

Landing numbers are however debateable as one former fisher fondly recalled campers at the beach waiting on the shore for a "fry" most evenings and whether these numbers were included in the landing record is uncertain.

The station operated a bag netting system with fixed bag nets (similar to a seine net) being mounted with leader nets on either site to guide the fish into the bag. The nets would have been fished a couple of times a day when the weather was good enough.

The system of fishing relied on the tides to bring the salmon along the coast and through the carefully placed nets.

The rifle was also an important piece of equipment in the station. Alongside the means to mend nets, it was to help deal with the biggest enemy of the salmon fisher – the harbour seal. Managing the seal population locally was one of the tasks that not everyone enjoyed, but was a key part of maintaining stocks.

Visitors today will notice the drying poles for the nets on the green where the nets were dried out of season and the leaders were hung on a Saturday evening to allow a rest on the Sabbath.

Sadly the station closed in the mid-1990s due to pressures on salmon stocks and local estates seeking to maximise the number of fish which made it into the rivers.

It was given a new lease of life when the local Historic Society and latterly the crofters restored the building for future generations.

The demise of fishing
(or not)

The death of George MacKay in a motor accident was a severe blow to Lochinver Fish Selling business in 1979. George was greatly respected, but many would say his greatest flaw was that he would never delegate a job he could do himself. When he was gone, there were many jobs that no-one else even knew he did.

One skipper recalled a boat which was a "summer visitor" to Lochinver and had no real connection with LFS. The boat had been struggling to compete with larger and more modern craft and was in her owner's view badly in need of some new equipment.

On hearing this, George offered to supply whatever they needed on the condition that they paid him back when they could from the profits they'd make using whatever he supplied.

The boat remained in Lochinver well into the Winter months that year (where it of course brought revenue both to the port and to LFS) with the skipper diligently putting a little bit aside every week from the boats earnings to pay off his debt.

Just before Christmas he walked into the LFS offices with a bundle of cash (as much of the business was done on a cash basis at the time) and was handed in return a bundle of weekly boat settlements with an underline on each to show where the company had paid itself from the boats outstanding debt.

The additional profit generated from having newer nets etc had been so good that the skipper hadn't even noticed the additional deductions on his weekly settlement.

It turned out that his debt had been paid in full a couple of months earlier. The whole crew enjoyed a decent Christmas bonus that year.

The story underlines the way the business operated to help the fishing community but perhaps also highlights that in the good times, there was a bonanza for the boats.

Some noted that in the weeks after his passing there were a few chaotic times and they felt they could trace a gradual decline in the harbour from then.

The reality though is that it is much more complex than that and there is probably no clear answer to when fishing began to decline or what the causes were. It was certainly apparent in interviews that the older the interviewee, the earlier they saw the demise beginning. One interviewee, though it was long before his own time, noted that there was perhaps a cycle of demise. This he noted began with a herring industry whose demise began before the First World War and between the wars fell to zero as the few remaining local boats switched to white fish. By the mid-1980s this resource was beginning to decline, and the fishers began to concentrate more on shellfish.

This oral tradition is supported by some early evidence. The Dalhousie Commission of 1883 was the third royal commission devoted to overfishing and noted that there was a falling off in flat fish takes in both quality and quality and that the North Sea was becoming "exhausted".

Legislation always comes up in discussions with the fishing community – Britain's entry into the Common Fisheries Policy in the early 1990s was seen by many as the opening of our waters (outside of 12 miles from the coast) to a much larger number of bigger craft and coupled with the quota system in the same legislation was never a popular piece of legislation.

An additional factor was the changes in technology. Throughout the 1960s and into the 1970s the predominant method of fishing was the seine net. The net crucially hung in the water rather than being dragged through it – except when being hauled in. Possibly a crucial factor in the demise of seine net fishing was that the crew were constantly at work – feeding the net out, hauling it in, separating, boxing, icing the fish and repeat. It is arguable that fish stocks had been declining throughout the 1960s and 1970s causing the seine net to become a marginal benefit – but when it was eventually replaced by the more damaging trawl, it also brought in an easier style of working.

The small area (room) covered by the seine (perhaps a few hundred metres in length at a maximum) was considerably smaller than that covered by a similar sized net being dragged along the bottom at 3 or 4 knots for several hours – at least a couple of fishers noted that those 9 or 10 miles of fishing were a lot more productive but also more damaging.

One interviewee felt that creation of fish farms was a huge factor in the demise of fish stocks. When they first started, there was little thought on how the fish would be fed. This led to a market for undersized fish – often with a premium price being paid – to be made into fish meal. Boats fishing the seine net were unable to capitalise on this and switched to the trawl where fish of all sizes would be scooped up in the net and there was a rapid switch to this method of fishing. However, taking the smaller fish damaged stocks and destroyed the sustainability of the Minch.

Some skippers were warning on this very early on and urging other skippers to return to the seine net, albeit with little success. Some felt that by the early 1980s catches were dropping rapidly and that by the time of quotas and decommissioning many skippers were more than happy to sell up as the fish were gone. This may have been exacerbated by larger boats with covered decks which were much less weather bound than the older boats.

During the 1970s as the trawl became predominant, the technique rolled the net along the bottom, scooping up everything in its way, which potentially destroyed the breeding grounds for young fish. This was exacerbated by the closed mesh on the net which scooped up the young fish also.

It is the loss of breeding grounds that many skippers felt quickly destroyed fish stocks and potential young stocks. The risk of snagging the net on underwater rocks also meant that skippers were prone to repeatedly re-trawling the same smoothed underwater highways. With a growing number of boats in the 1970s, this meant that more and more marginal (often inside the 3-mile limit) grounds were being fished which compounded the issues.

Some suggest that the trawl was just a factor and it combined with the ever increasing size and capacity of the boats to catch more.

Skipper's wife Jean McBain was one of the more senior people spoken with and confirmed that in her husband's early days most of the boats were in the 30-40 feet length and that her husband craft, the "Golden Emblem" was at 55 feet one of the bigger boats when it first was built. By the mid 1970s though many of the boats were perhaps another 15 feet longer and certainly today, some boats landing in Lochinver are in excess of 150 feet in length. With the larger frame comes more powerful engines, winches, bigger nets, and larger catches which might suggest evidence of a belief that this is a major factor in the decline of stocks.

It is certainly true that landings delivered by modern trawlers far exceed anything a single boat would have managed in previous generations.

One of the factors fishers had to content with was the 3-mile limit which was introduced by the Cameron report in 1970 and prohibited the use of mobile gear within three miles of the shore. It was observed to a point and policed. Some found ways around it and some ignored it at every opportunity.

Lochinver was known for its plaice and buyers from all over the country and the North of England were often seen looking for them. One fisher knowing that they preferred the shallow waters was known to agree with other local boatowners on a day when they would lift their anchors in Loch Roe, so that he could run a quick trawl up the length of the loch – well inside the 3-mile exclusion zone of course.

One tale suggests that a skipper well known for fishing inside the limits was overheard in conversation with a Stoer crofter whether he thought the boat was fishing closer to the shore than the limits allowed.

The reply was "Three-mile limit? You could have reached over the side and pulled my tatties".

The boats all had radios and regularly communicated with one another while at sea. The radios worked on a number of different channels. If a fisheries protection vessel was spotted, it would prompt a series messages to relay where it was, where it was heading and how fast – meaning anyone fishing inside the limits would have more than enough time to lift their gear and reposition themselves a little further from the shore.

There were, of course, those that were happy to report "poaching" inside the limit and conversely, those that built their careers on it.

One fisher noted that between the radio communications and the tell-tale black smoke the arrival of the fisheries protection vessel could be anticipated while it was miles away. It usually wasn't an issue, but once the spotter plane arrived on the scene, things got more difficult.

The three-mile limit also caused issues with creel fishers – particularly when a trawler ran a net right over their creels and at one stage crofters on Lewis were taking exception to all this poaching in Broad Bay to the point that there were reports of some shots being fired from the shore.

One Lochinver based boat was doing just that and whilst a crewmember was scooping fish in the fish pound at the side of the wheelhouse, his skipper chucked his cigarette end out of the window hitting the poor crewman on the back of his neck.

With all the rumours of shots being fired, the man in question felt the burn on his neck and immediately assumed the crofter shotgun was to blame.

Help I've been shot he shouted. Lossie museum has a poem on the wall celebrating this event.

Radio communications were of course not limited to tipping each other off about approaching fishery protection vessels. Weather reports, changes in the swell of the water and some of the boats had ties with particular buyers and would let them know in a coded radio message if they had a good haul.

Fishery protection vessel (credit: Morag Maclennan)

The radio channels were open and skippers were never keen to let anyone else know where they got a good haul for fear of losing the chance to return for more, but buyers would be travelling from as far afield as Aberdeen and it was important that they knew that it was worth their while to make the drive. It was crucial for the buyers to be aware of normal trip lengths, weather conditions and when several of the larger boats were likely to land on the same night – more fish normally meant a higher chance of a lower price.

When the quota system was introduced – something you would struggle to find a fisher with a good word to say about. Most note that when you trawl a net behind a boat you cannot put out a shopping list with it. What fish are caught, are caught and after being dragged behind a boat for several hours are almost certainly dead.

This led to something of a stand-off – once a quota number had been reached, either dead fish could be dumped over the side, or it could be sold illegally for cash in so called "black landings".

It is easy to understand why these would happen. There can be little more soul destroying than after hours of dangerous toil having to ditch your rewards and throw dead fish over the side. Ecologically the policy did nothing for fish stocks:

"A fishing boat isn't like a supermarket. You can't just stick a shopping list on the side of a net and ask for 'no cod today' – you catch what you catch"

When quotas came in there was less evidence of black fish landings in Lochinver (when compared to other ports) but it did happen. Crews would wait until the harbour office closed and land straight into the back of a truck. Though no one interviewed admitted their own involvement, there was always a story of someone else who was breaking the rules and with it came some interesting stories:

A harbour worker recalled one occasion when the port authority arrived in the middle of the night after being tipped off and found a lorry loaded with illegal fish. He went to call for backup and demanded that the vehicle would not be moved. Harbour workers were only too happy to comply, but as he had only said the lorry could not be moved, they were able in the 10 minutes or so that he was away to procure another vehicle, move everything into it and hide it well away from the scene. As no fish could be found, no charges could be brought.

In a similar story, one of the many duties the port authority had was to register catches and where they had been caught.

Unfortunately, many fishers had their own secret spots that they shared with no-one for fear that others would clean them out, so they were always reticent to share these. That was always going to be an issue with the law.

One fisherman, in particular, when fishing perfectly legally was unwilling to give a precise location for his catch on one night. He was incensed that "the minch" was not clear enough for the harbour officer.

The harbour officer was equally adamant that an entire channel of water covering ever piece of mainland North of Skye out to the Outer Hebrides was far from clear enough.

The shouting match went on for some time and a local mechanic caught in the middle could only watch on in embarrassment until the harbour officer stormed off, pulled down the roller doors in the harbour building they were in and locked the two of them inside.

One skipper regularly sent his two sons across the village to sit on the wall of a friend's house and watch for the lights in the harbour office and the police station to both go out – as soon as they did, they would be back at the harbour for a second landing. This was confirmed by the friend who recalled the lads often popping over for a cup of tea, but never coming inside for fear of "leaving scales on the furniture".

Throughout the 1990s government subsidies were available to decommission your boats. Older skippers with no-one willing to take on their craft were struggling to compete with newer and larger trawlers and were only too happy to do so. Similar subsidies were offered to boats who wished to convert to creel fishing and one or two were able to take advantage of both.

In parallel with this, deals were being struck with European business both to package and supply shell fish and for continental trawlers to land in Lochinver.

This came to a head in 1992 with the opening of the new harbour extension where skippers noted loading bays were designed to easier accommodate right hand drive (continental) lorries. A blockade of Lochinver bay was organised to prevent any continental boats landing at the harbour.

One fisher recalled with a smile that several of the continental boats had already landed before the protest started and not only were the crews in the bar during the protest, they were later joined in a game of pool by some of the men returning from protesting against them.

State of fishing today (2021)

There is little doubt that the harbour extension in the 1990s was an enabler for larger continental boats to fish from Lochinver and little doubt that this trade over the past 25 years or more has helped create and maintain jobs in the port.

Today the vast majority of landings at the port are made by continental boats and the majority of their catch travels to the continent.

Current Lochinver harbour (credit: John C. MacLeod)

The harbour extension has transformed the port and it is unrecognisable from the one of even 40 years ago.

Landings are surprisingly close to the peak years, but of course these boats fish much further from home and land less frequently.

Breton trawler Jean Claude Coulon (credit: John C. MacLeod)

APPENDIX 1

BOATS WHICH FISHED FROM LOCHINVER

With thanks to John C. MacLeod for this list of boats which he recalls fishing at Lochinver in the 1960s and 1970s – there are omissions including his own Celestial Dawn (which may have been later than the list), but it gives a good indication of some of the many craft we remember fondly and I am hopeful will remind readers of others to add.

Lochinver Fishing Fleet from 1960 onwards

INVERLOSSIE UL 106
1957   Built J. Noble, Fraserburgh.
1972   Sold to Sandy Mackenzie, January 1972, Lossiemouth, became Ranger UL 106.
1976   Sold to Orkney.
Notes   68 feet. Skipper Wullie John Farquhar. Painted green when new.

COLINNE UL160
1958   Built Jones Buckie.
1976   Sold to Fleetwood.
Notes   70 feet (big able boat). Skipper Tommy Gault, then Alex Scott (Balmoral), then James Stewart, then Sandy Gault (Sandy was skipper twice I think). First boat in Lochinver to fit a radar (big white scanner).

BEN LOYAL UL 166
1960 Built by Herd and Mackenzie, Peterhead.
1977 Sold to Wick - new number WK 3.
Notes 70 feet (big able boat with very good beam). Skipper John Stewart.

GOLDEN EMBLEM UL 135
c1956 Built Macduff.
1986 Sold.
Notes Approx 50 feet. Skipper David McBain then Alex McBain.

VALHALLA UL 55
c1954 Built by Millar St. Monance.
1972 Sold to Wick.
Notes Approx 55 feet. Skipper Duncan Sutherland.

OLIVE LEAF INS 54 (front of pic).
1958 Built by Herd and Mackenzie, Buckie.
1974 Sunk on striking Proudfoot Rocks going into Wick.
Notes 70 feet (bg boat with wide beam, thought it was the best boat). In Lochinver Skipper Campbell Thomson. Replaced by Olive Leaf INS 128. Which was previously registered in Banff as the Marguerita. Replaced by Moravia INS 86. Built 1975 Herd and Mackenzie.

CALEDONIA INS 311

1956 Built by Herd and Mackenzie, Buckie.
1969 Sold to Ireland replaced with Horizon INS 21.
Notes 70 feet. Skipper John Thomson. Used
to be most often the last boat to finish on a
Thursday.

DAYSTAR INS 317

1954 Built by Noble, Fraserburgh.
1971 Sold to Wick. Became Daystar WK 84
for at least ten years.
Notes Approx 60 feet. Sharp bow, made it
narrow forward. Skipper Eddie Farquhar.

STARONIA INS 273

1954 Built by Macduff Boatbuilding Co.
1969 Sold to Fraserburgh.
Notes 65 feet. Skipper John Gault.

ATLANTIS INS 73

1956 Built by Jones, Buckie.
1974 Sold to Plymouth.
Notes 65 feet. Skipper Jim Soutar.

SUBLIME INS 557

1949 Built by Macduff Boatbuilding Co.
1973 Sold to Fleetwood.
Notes 65 feet. Skipper Mitchell Gault.
New casing added probably by Herd and
Mackenzie with galley door on port side.
Converted to trawling.

NORTHERN MAID INS 42

1957 Built by Jones, Buckie.
1980 Sold to Alex Brown, renamed Ocean Gleaner INS 42.
Notes Approx 68 feet (narrow boat). Skipper Simon Soutar.

BALMORAL INS 45

1957 Built by Thomson Buckie.
1970 Sunk after collision with Gem in North Sea.
Notes 65 feet. Skipper Alex Scott.

KITTIWAKE INS 232

1946 Built by Macduff Boatbuilding Co.
1969 Sold to Ireland.
Notes Approx 58 feet. Skipper George Thomson.

INCENTIVE INS 155

1955 Built by Herd and Mackenzie.
1974 Sold to Ian Smith, Buckie, then Fleetwood.
1982 Went ashore on Kirkaig Point.
Notes 65 feet (narrow beam). Skipper Bouff! Then Sandy Smith Lossiemouth. Replaced with Vigilant SY 28 became Vigilant UL 55 for the next 30 Years. Replaced with Loch Erisort SY 434.

TUDOR ROSE INS 284

1955 Built by Tommy Summers.
1970 Sold to Peterhead.
Notes 63 feet. Skipper Wullie John Farquhar then Josie Penny (Campbell).

ARCADIA INS 207

1957 Built by Thomson Buckie.
1983 Went ashore on Stoer Head.
Notes 65 feet. Same model of boat as Balmoral and Leander. Skipper Alex Flett.

SPINAWAY INS 206

1955 Built by Macduff Boatbuilding Co.
c1967 Replaced by the Sapphire UL 194.
Notes 65 feet (a big able boat possibly 70 foot). Skipper Jimmy Gault. Sapphire built as Gulliemot INS 304 by Herd and Mackenzie, Buckie.

RISING SEA BCK 206

1949 Built by Thomson, Buckie.
1968 Replaced by Ilene BCK 2.
Notes Rebuilt with new casing by Herd and Mackenzie. Skipper John Smith snr, Andrew Smith, George Smith then Iain Smith.

OLIVE LEAF BCK 210

1948 Built.
Notes Skipper Old John Smith then George Smith.

OLYMPIC INS 16
1956 Built by Jones, Buckie.
1977 Sold to Eyemouth.
Notes Approx 63 feet. This boat had several different skippers including J. Young, Hopeman, Benji Scott, Sandy Gault, Jimmy Campbell (Covesea), Dennis Slater, Stuart Jones. I believe was in Lochinver when new with Tommy Gault as skipper.

GUIDE ON INS 70
1946 Built.
1980 Sold to Aberdeen.
Notes 65 feet, same boat as Incentive INS 155. Do not know when started working Lochinver. Skipper Beam Campbell.

GIRL WILMA INS 53
c1954 Built by Summers of Fraserburgh.
1968 Sold.
1975 Sold from Lossiemouth as Cairngorm INS 53.
Notes 60 feet, this boat was not in Lochinver all the time just spells as I remember.
Skipper Sandy Mackenzie. Skipper David.
Re-named Cairngorm INS 53. This boat would have made a good prawn trawler, a better size than some of the boats who worked the prawn trawl in the seventies.

Then in the summertime for spells

FAME INS 56
1957 Built in Banff.
1984 Decommisioned.
Notes 65 feet (narrow boat). Last boat to be built in Banff. Skipper Alex Ralph. Just in Lochinver for a short period now and again in the sixties. A well kept boat converted to a prawn trawler.

LEANDER INS 72
1957 Built by Thomson, Buckie
1980 Sold to Ireland.
Notes Approx 68 feet. Just in Lochinver short spells. Skipper A. Campbell then 1975 Eddie Fiske. Regular in Lochinver. Adam Main.

Other boats, which I cannot remember only told or in pictures

SPEEDWELL INS 164

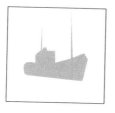

AVONDALE INS 201
Built Macduff Boatbuilding Co, same as Staronia). There was a man who worked in Lossiemouth Fishermans mission who used to tell me he was four years in the Avondale out of Lochinver.

JEANNIE MACKAY WK

MARANATHA

VALMARK

VISION

Boats that I remember in Lochinver - Mid 1960s, for a summer working through the night

FRUITFUL BOUGH INS 269
Approx 63 feet. Built by Thomson, Buckie.

OCEAN GLEANER INS 42
Approx 65 feet. Built by Herd and Mackenzie.
Same boat as Guide On and Incentive.
Skippers were brothers Alex and John Ralph.

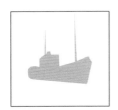

ATHENA INS 334
New Boat c1960 for a summer, or a couple of
years. This boat had a herring hatch so deck a bit
cramped with seine net ropes. Skipper Ian Flett.

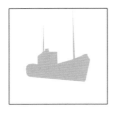

WAVE SHEAF INS 118
Built by Noble, Fraserburgh. Skipper
E.Thomson. Big Green Painted boat. Lovely
new boat. Became Marradale BCK 223.
Then the Heroine INS 158, renamed Palm INS
158 (Built c1956, Macduff Boatbuilding Co.)
started working from Lochinver about 1967.
Skipper Mike Campbell.

Then in 1965 the new built boats

COVESEA INS 307
1975 Sold to Lossiemouth became Shannon INS 307.
Notes 60 foot. Built by Herd and Mackenzie. Skipper Jimmy Campbell.

VICTORY INS 224
1975 Sold to Burghead or Hopeman, renamed Embrace.
Notes 60 foot. Built by Herd and Mackenzie. Skipper Bill Fennell. 1970 Skipper Bob Soutar.

DIADEM INS 154
1973 Sold to Ayr - Freedom BA 280.
Notes 60 foot. Built by Thomson, Buckie. Skipper Thomson Fiske.

SUNRISE UL 66
65 feet. Built by Herd and Mackenzie. Skipper John Campbell then Benji Scott, later Charlie Coull. Hydraulic Power Block and Sutherland Belt Driven Combination Seine Net Winch.

HORIZON INS 21
75 feet, Built by Herd and Mackenzie. Caterpillar Engine, Jensen Combination Winch Whaleback. Replaced Caledonia. Skipper John Thomson.

FIONAGAL INS 67

Painted green. Later Sunbeam INS 67, painted black. 65 feet. Noble, Fraserburgh for a period before going to work from Peterhead. Skipper Bill Smith.

OCEAN GLEANER INS 200

J. Davidson as skipper. Seine net boat later converted to trawling for prawns.

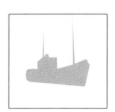

CASTLE VALE N12

1956 Built as Havilah was also N12 by Herd and Mackenzie. Skipper John Young from Hopeman then Sandy Gault. Hull painted Baltic Blue.

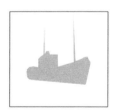

DILIGENCE INS 188

1940s Built.
Seine net boat first then Prawn Trawler. Skipper A. Duthrie.

TORFNESS INS 164.

Older boat with new wheelhouse and sharp stern. 1970 or 1971 for one summer, Burghead boat. Went home for a paint at end of summer and did not come back.

BOUNTY BF 7

Approx 70 foot. Sputnik Trawler converted to seine net. Red Hull with Blue deck. Operated for one summer about 1970. Came back on Sunday and stayed out until Thursday.

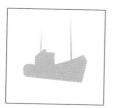

STRATHNAIRN INS 176
1956 Built Jones, Buckie
Notes Approx 65 Feet.
Nairn boat just sometimes for a short time in the autumn. Earlier version of the Northern Maid. Could have been after 1970.

CARONIA INS 146
1954 Built Herd and Mackenzie.
Notes Approx 68 foot. Skipper Alex Flett after 1971. Worked out of Lochinver for a short period in the autumn.

OSPREY INS 142
Skipper John Crocket. Old boat do not know how long trawled out of Lochinver. Nearly ended up on Cruamer during a storm, with Elmgrove BCK114.

ENTERPRISING INS 11
Built T. Summers about 55 foot, good handy-sized smaller boat. A few weeks one summer.

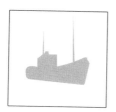

ENDEAVOUR INS 295
1954 Built by Thomson.
Think one summer.

MAYFLOWER INS 35
Saw this boat in Lochinver for one weekend when there was a good fishing I expect.

APPENDIX 2

FISHING BOAT EVENTS

Event

Several Seine Net boats drifting below our house at Baddidarroch, could recognise the Kittiwake and could hear late Roddy Reharn shouting instructions as they were towed back to the pier. Probably shifted for the tide from in front of the Culag Bar for them to be afloat when the crews came back on Sunday and not secured properly.

Event

1967- Week before Games Day-1967 or 1966.

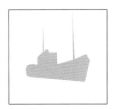

BRITANNIA INS 68

1956 Built by Thomson.

Event Went ashore on Stoer, towed in by Inverlossie on the Wednesday morning at low tide. When tide came in went to top of pier and waited for good weather until Saturday. Games Day that Friday, boat at top of pier with blue tarpaulin over stem post and part of bow. Hull painted Grey. Sailed for Lossie on the Saturday.

Event

1970 Inverlossie struck by fishing boat going out to sea on stern post and partly sunk, towed around in front of Culag Bar but tide was out so beached opposite Ice plant and Culag Bar. Would have cost to repair and a loss of fishing time, perhaps a factor in the boat being sold soon afterwards. Some of these boats worked the deep water in the North Minch landing whiting and small fish, some like the Olive Leaf INS 54 worked the North Grounds and North Rona, Sule Skier, Flannens, Butt of Lewis etc.

It is said there were fifty boats in Lochinver, in the sixties, mainly by incomers, I do not think so, at least not in the sixties anyway, probably more like twenty five. There was a very good fleet of mainly Lossiemouth INS registered boats, mostly around sixty five feet long, with the UL registered Lossiemouth crewed Fish Selling Co. partly owned boats and the two Smith BCK registered boats, built late fifties mostly, with the two locally owned boats around fifty feet long.

There was a lot of coming and going, some boats for the summer fishing, in the winter there would be Herring Drifters lying until dark, Avoch Ringers anchored in the bay which we would see on our way to school. Sometimes Mallaig Lobster Boats in for shelter.

During the Seventies there were a lot of SY registered boats landing in Lochinver on Tuesdays and Thursdays.

In 1980s there were nearly fifty boats but only for a few weekends in the spring. However the boats covered a big range from some seventy feet long, (Motor Fishing Vessels), built during the War to small creel boats.

A lot of them were by then, old obsolete boats, mainly registered BCK or BF displaced from Herring and White Fish Fishing, and nothing like the sixties fleet.

The sixties fleet was purpose built for the Seine Net Fishing with nearly new boats with mostly young fit crews. These boats worked from Sunday Night until Thursday. The eighties fleet were some new bigger boats, working from Sunday until Thursday built for working further out, but mostly old obsolete boats, converted from seine net fishing for whitefish or Herring Drift Net fishing to Prawn Trawling working the slack tide for Ten Day Trips with a lot of the crews just putting in the time until retirement...